T0316679

KARL MARX'S *DAS KAPITAL* EXPLAINED

KARL MARX'S *DAS KAPITAL* EXPLAINED

SEUNGSOO LIM

Algora Publishing
New York

Library of Congress Cataloging-in-Publication Data —

Library of Congress Cataloging-in-Publication Data

Names: Lim, Seungsoo, 1975- author.
Title: Karl Marx's Das Kapital explained / Seungsoo Lim, Heejong Kwon,
    translator.
Description: New York : Algora Publishing, 2019. | Summary: "This is a
    lucid step-by-step guide to Karl Marx's Das Kapital for all the readers of
    the world. Its treatment of the content of Das Kapital pivots on the
    classroom exchanges between a lecturer and his students"-- Provided by
    publisher.
Identifiers: LCCN 2019020170 (print) | LCCN 2019980834 (ebook) | ISBN
    9781628943894 (paperback) | ISBN 9781628943900 (hardcover) | ISBN
    9781628943917 (pdf)
Subjects: LCSH: Capital. | Economics. | Marx, Karl, 1818-1883--Political
    and social views.
Classification: LCC HB501 .L496 2019 (print) | LCC HB501 (ebook) | DDC
    335.4/12--dc23
LC record available at https://lccn.loc.gov/2019020170
LC ebook record available at https://lccn.loc.gov/2019980834

Front Cover: Karl Marx, 1861,
                Source: *Reminiscences of Carl Schurz*, by Richard Beard, Vol. I,
                New York: McClure Publ. Co., 1907, Chap. 4, facing p. 170.

Printed in the United States

Table of Contents

INTRODUCTION

Das Kapital by Karl Marx: How do people react to this book title? There may be various responses, but most of them fall into one of three categories:

Reaction 1: "I'm not interested in Socialism or Communism."

Reaction 2: "Who would read such an outdated book?"

Reaction 3: "I guess it's interesting, but it's long and hard to read; I'd never get through it."

I'll discuss each as we go along, but to begin with, let's clear up a few misunderstandings inherent in these responses.

First, the title of the book Karl Marx wrote is *Das Kapital*, that is, *Capital*.

What Marx was examining was neither Socialism nor Communism, but how Capitalism functions. His book is long, indeed, but from beginning to end, it focuses on how Capitalism works. And no matter how hard you look, you won't find anything in the book that has to do with Socialism or Communism.

Reaction 2 is based on a different misunderstanding. When

it came out 150 years ago, the book was an uncontested first. Karl Marx (1818–1883) was remarkably prescient. The trends he identified have been documented on a grand scale and they are even destructive across the globe in our times. It doesn't take much imagination to transpose the problems he discussed to the economic and social environment that continues to evolve before our eyes.

Reaction 3 is not a misunderstanding at all.

Honestly, anybody confronting *Capital* for the first time is bound to feel overwhelmed by the sheer quantity of information in this 3-volume work, its strange vocabulary, and the complex sentences. And most of those who have the courage to start reading *Capital* end up putting it down, running into a brick wall with Part I, "Commodities and Money". It's just what any high school student might do: you dare to tackle a difficult study guide, but only the early part of it alone gets any attention.

This book is written to address that last concern. Here, we reorganize the kernel of *Capital* into an easy-to-understand dialogue. The book presents formulas once in a while, but nothing to worry about. Four operations are all the calculation needed, and I've solved them all for you. Anyone who reads *Capital* in the short bits of time carved out of their daily rat race could grasp this kernel in just a week. With passion and will, you can finish it in one day.

Of course, the book doesn't go into all the details included in the three volumes of *Das Kapital*. If reading this book gets you more interested, I recommend that you go ahead and read all *Das Kapital*. Perhaps, after this introduction, you'll be able to breeze through it and enjoy it more.

This book doesn't talk about *Das Kapital* only. To help readers understand the context, I add my views which don't stray far from the original. I hope readers will understand this as it is to ensure a more effective delivery of *Das Kapital*.

As luck has it, I taught a college-level course on Capitalism for six years, focusing on Marxist analysis. At first, I wondered if any students would take an elective on Marxism, but the course grew from a small seminar to a 200-student lecture format. I've had goosebumps when reading class assignments submitted by students. I have felt the shock that students experience at their first exposure to Karl Marx's analysis of capitalism.

While explaining the Marxist perspective to students, I became sure of one thing. The question is not whether Marxist philosophy is out of date but *What does it have to do with us?* The change in students' perceptions that I've witnessed is stark. Today, when the dysfunctionalities, disparities and wealth inequality in Western society are intensifying, why shouldn't we go back and re-acquaint ourselves with a classic analysis of the causes and consequences of the inner workings of the capitalist economic system? Marxist theory is highly relevant.

In 2005, BBC conducted a survey in the UK. When it asked experts to choose the world's most well-known and influential thinkers, Karl Marx came in first. By contrast, in Korea people continue to suffer from the national partition based on an ideological face-off. There is no opportunity to learn about Marxist philosophy as part of the regular curriculum without a massive distortion or demonization. South Koreans may not be the only ones. I hope that the discussion in these pages will provide a better understanding of the Marxist analysis of the capitalist system for readers who are interested.

This book was first published in South Korea in 2008 and has established itself as a guide to *Das Kapital* through its several revised editions. I thank my readers for their constructive and positive feedback. I also thank Heejong Kwon, who did a tremendous job translating the work into English. I want to express my heart-felt thanks to Algora Publishing for providing unstinting support in publishing this South Korean author's book in English. I am grateful to everyone who is related to this book. But my special thanks go to my wife and two daughters. I can't thank them enough for living happily with me despite my shortcomings.

This is a critical period in which capitalism is facing a crisis due to serious depression and a glaring, growing gap between rich and poor as well as increasing unemployment. So, my greatest hope is that this book will help readers understand the nature of capitalism and work on alternatives.

Seungsoo Lim
Like a farmer who sows seeds

Lecture 1 — Why Should We Study *Das Kapital*?

Lecturer: Hello, everyone. Nice to meet you. As our class has more than 200 students, we'll skip the roll call. It's surprising and even odd to see this large a number of students enrolled in a lecture on *Das Kapital* (Capital). I particularly find it impressive that we have a lot of students who major in Economics or Business. And I want to hear why you've chosen this course. Anyone?

Student A: I'm an Economics major. We only learn mainstream economics at our department. So, I wanted to try a different perspective on capitalism. A senior who took this course told me that the lecture was shocking; it entirely changed his view of capitalism.

Student B: I'm a Sociology major. In our other coursework, we sometimes come across the name of Marx, but I realized that I don't know much about Marx. Then, I saw this course and I hopped in.

Lecturer: I see. When I first offered this course, I thought that it would appeal mostly to student activists. But, as a matter of fact, I don't have many of them in my class. Of course, we don't have many activists these days on campus...

Student C: Well, Professor, I'm taking the class because in my opinion, capitalist society has a lot of problems, countless issues including an enormous gap between rich and poor, environmental destruction, and the belief that money means everything. I heard that in *Das Kapital*, Marx presented quite a logical and scientific analysis of capitalist society. That's why I added this course.

Criticizing Das Kapital *without knowing its content*

Lecturer: Well, it's clear that you've all chosen this course for various reasons and you're driven by different goals. In fact, most people shy away from someone who brings up Marx's *Das Kapital*. You know what's so funny? If you ask those people what *Das Kapital* is about, they say they don't know. Yet, even though they don't know anything about the book, people are quick to criticize the book for being irrelevant.

Student D: I think most people have the impression that the book discusses Socialism and Communism. And, people think that capitalism dominates while Socialism and Communism are unrealistic models and have failed.

Lecturer: Right. And yet, *Das Kapital* isn't a book that talks about Socialism or Communism. It talks about Capitalism! It presents a systematic and scientific analysis of capitalism, the social/economic system we belong to. And the book has earned its fame thanks to the sharp analysis it presents. Nevertheless, a lot of people associate *Das Kapital* with Socialism and Communism and dismiss it as obsolete.

Student E: Exactly. When I say I'm taking this course, my friends say, "What, are you some kind of commie activist?" And most students are focused on getting jobs or starting a business and they don't give a damn about social issues or broader ideas. By the way, I understand that you were an Engineering major, Professor.

Lecturer: Right. I was an Engineering major. And that's perhaps why I'm glad to meet STEM students in my class. Students who are here today have enrolled in the course for various reasons, but one thing seems clear. If this capitalist world were going forward flawlessly, there wouldn't be so much interest in this course.

So, what's the reality? The gap between rich and poor is widening. And while problems experienced by temporary workers are a big issue, companies don't want to hire more full-time workers. A lot of young people who have graduated from colleges can't get a job. People are so enthralled by money that some even commit murder. If you take a close look at environmental degeneration and industrial disasters, they often occur because companies want to increase their profits and so they fail to install waste water filtering equipment or use safety devices. And even then, when such problems occur, people have come to think of them as natural in any society.

Student F: Schools don't treat such grave issues seriously. If you take a course in Economics, you hear that it's because the market is temporarily off balance between demand and supply. And they explain that they can solve the problem by letting the invisible hand take care of it. And they just keep solving all those calculus equations. But I've never seen an economic formula that cogently explains problems like the income gap, the lack of adequate employment opportunities, environmental degradation, industrial accidents, wars, and famine. I don't see how they can result from "a slight deviation from the balance between demand and supply."

Why do we need to understand Das Kapital *now?*

Lecturer: It's a tough life in the real world. When people ask me why they should know Marx's *Das Kapital* at this point, I tell them to look at this world. I ask, does this capitalist world look beautiful to you? If you think this is the best we can do, you don't have to study *Das Kapital*. You can live your life as you have done so far. However, if you want to know what makes you feel terrible and helpless about all the many problems inherent in a capitalist society, you're ready for it.

Student H: If I can understand *Das Kapital*, will I really know what's causing these problems? It's such a famous classic, I'm interested to know what it says, but I don't expect too much of it. When there is a problem that so many people haven't succeeded in solving, it's hard to believe that the cause of the problem was already laid out in a proper analysis in a book that came out 150 years ago.

Lecturer: You'll have to hear the lecture to see whether you can find the cause of the problem or not. Or, you can attend the lecture, thinking that you're just reading a good classic.

My introduction has been a bit too long. Let's go to the main part of the lecture.

What is capitalism?

Lecturer: We're living in a so-called capitalist society. So, let's think. What kind of society is a capitalist society? I'll give you about 20 seconds, and you can write down your definition in your notebook.

(A while later) Now, take the sheet out of your notebook and hand it in. Let's see what you've all come up with.

A society run as a market economy
A liberal democracy
A money-centered society
A jungle-like society
A work-exploiting society
A society where rich people are happy
A society where poor people are sad
A society where the rich–poor gap keeps widening
An industrial society with advanced technology
A society where values are calculated as money
A society that converts everything to commodities
A society made up of capitalists and workers

Lecturer: Well, what kind of definition is that? Pretty vague, isn't it?

To get a better idea what are the important features of a capitalist society, we need to compare it with the other social-economic structures that have existed in history. In much of the world, people have gone through most of these stages of development:

- Primitive communist society

- Slavery

- Feudalism

- Capitalism

- Socialism

- Communist Society

What would be the criteria for distinguishing various social-economic formations?

Relations of production are what differentiates social-economic formations

Student A: Well, I've never thought about that. Hmmm, does a person's social position change? A slave becomes a feudal tenant, and then a citizen... I'm not sure.

Lecturer: Don't feel discouraged. While 'social position' is not entirely accurate, that was a pretty good answer. But let me tell you the answer: The best criterion for distinguishing different types of social-economic organization is the 'relations of production'. Let's talk about it.

People have to eat to survive. Moreover, people have to wear clothes and need a house to live in. In modern society we need not only basic necessities but also a number of goods such as television, cell phone, washing machine, medical instruments, and a car. But goods that we need in our life don't appear out of nowhere. Some people work to make them.

In this sense, work is essential to human survival and existence in a society. Many people work, participating in the production activities as members of the community. And relations of production, which are created among people, differ greatly with social formations.

Slave-owner–slave: The relations of production in a slave society

Lecturer: For example, in a slave society, people who participate in production activities relate with one another either as slaves or slave-owners. "Relations of production" in a slave society are between slaves and slave-owners. Slaves are priced and sold, like things, to slave-owners. And they're run and worked like animals or machines, as instructed by slave-owners. In a slave society, slave-owners who accumulate wealth by running slaves make up the ruling class that dominates the society.

Lord–serf: The relations of production in a feudal society

Then, how about a feudal society? In mediaeval Europe, feudal lords owned large tracts of land called manors; and serfs (also called tenant farmers, or villeins), were land-bound. They belonged to the manors, and made their living by farming a small part of the land to feed themselves and their families. They did not have the right to leave the piece of land they were assigned to. The serfs didn't own the land; they couldn't sell it or rent it out. But if the lord sold the land they were assigned to, they were part of the sale. And if they worked three days a week for their own benefit on the enfeoffed land, they worked another three days on the lord's estate, for his benefit, or they were obliged to hand over a large portion of their harvest to him.

So, the lord–serf relations of production are formed. This enabled the lords to accumulate wealth.

Capitalist–worker: The relations of production in a capitalist society

In a capitalist society, most people *sell* their labor power to people like capitalists, making a living by doing what they want them to do. We call them *workers*. Unlike workers, capitalists have *capital*, seed money for business. With the money, they buy land, build factories, acquire machines, and hire workers. They sell in the market products made at factories to make profits and thereby expand the size of the companies. Workers receive wages from capitalists.

In small companies, the capitalists are usually individuals, or perhaps families, investing their own savings and borrowing from the bank in their own name. They may take on partners to get more money to invest. As the company grows, more investors are needed to fuel the expansion. They're called shareholders. Large shareholders may include banks and other institutions, investment funds, and other wealthy families. Corporations often invest in each other's stock, too. Corporate CEOs represent them, working in their interests, for their benefit.

We mean all of these when we talk about the role of the *capi-*

talist, but another term is 'the One Percent.' In the last phase of capitalism as identified by Marx, the smaller players have been eliminated and the wealth has been concentrated in the hands of very few. In other words, the concentration of wealth is extreme. Today, we see that the vast majority of economic power is in the hands of 1% (actually, far less) of the society.

Thus, in a capitalist society, productive activity is carried out through 'capitalist–worker relations'. This is called 'the capitalist relations of production'. Most people sell their labor power to make a living. Those who can't get a job are in a bind. For this reason, workers are always at a disadvantage in their relationships with capitalists.

In America, for instance, people enter a worker–capitalist relationship for their productive activity, and we call it a capitalist society.

Now you've got some idea. Of course, a capitalist society has various complex aspects and cannot be adequately summarized as just the relations of production between workers and capitalists; but in a capitalist society the worker–capitalist relationship is the main axis of its productive activity.

Social formations and the situation of working people

Lecturer: Of course, a society can have several relations of production at the same time. For example, before the Civil War, the United States had a growing capitalist structure in the North with some slavery still being practiced, while slave-holding was the dominant form in the South. After the Civil War, the South moved toward a landlord–tenant relationship, that is, a kind of feudal relations of production, up until World War II. Tenants could rent land from a landowner and work to raise crops, paying their rent out of the harvest. Nonetheless, one could hardly call America a feudal society on that basis.

In defining a socio-economic formation, it is crucial to figure out its *dominant relations of production*. America is a capitalist society, because the capitalist relations of production dominate it. When talking about relations of production, there's one thing that we must mention. There are people who work hard in every society. They're working people who have held several names such as slaves, serfs, or workers. And we should pay attention to what kind of treatment they received in the past and in what situation they're in at the present.

In a slave society, working people were slaves and subjected to subhuman treatment. Slave-owners traded slaves like objects. They put slaves to forced labor while beating them with something like a whip, and provided them with minimum necessities needed to maintain their ability to work. Meanwhile, all the results of slaves' labor became the possessions of slave-owners. A good-natured slave-owner perhaps took a good care of the slaves, but the essence of the relationship remained the same.

Now let me ask you. Who was richer in a slave society, slaves or slave-owners?

Student B: Slave-owners, of course. Isn't it just logical? Slave-owners took everything that came from slaves' hard work.

Lecturer: That's right. Was my question too stupid? Let's suppose that 200 students in this course are all my slaves. Then, I should be able to make easy money. If I make you work for convenience stores and transfer $50 to my account each day, how much do I make a day? 200 times $50 per day makes a whopping $10,000 a day. Making $10,000 each day, I'm rich. Meanwhile, because you lose the compensation for your hard work, you get poorer.

Lecturer: Then, is the gap between rich and poor in a slave society caused by different abilities of individuals? Or is it because of social structure?

Student C: It's social structure, of course. Division of a society between slaves and slave-owners gives rise to a gap between rich and poor.

Lecturer: How about the life of serfs, the working people in the feudal society? Perhaps, their situation was a bit better than that of slaves. Serfs were not sold and bought like slaves, and manors had enfeoffed land where they could have their farming and were allowed to dispose of produce. Still, they weren't free from structural exploitation.

Let's say serfs worked six days a week, three days on their enfeoffed land and three days on a manor. Serfs must have been aware that working on one's own kitchen garden was quite different from working on their lord's land. While the produce from their kitchen garden was his, whatever he produced on the lord's land was going to be the lord's.

Here, let me try the convenience store analogy I used with regard to slave society. It's like paying $25 out of your daily pay of $50 and keeping the remaining $25 to yourself. By steadily collecting $25 from each of 200 students, I should get rich without fail, right? Meanwhile, your life would remain pretty hard. This is how exploitation works in a feudal society. And it's why feudalism too left a severe gap between rich and poor.

Then, what do we see in our capitalist society? In the current capitalist society, working people enjoy freedoms in their life that are incomparable to what was allowed to slaves or serfs. Capitalists and workers are equal human beings before the law. They appear equal as they receive the income due them from their respective economic activities. Nevertheless, the gap between rich and poor is enormous. The huge disparity between *the One Percent* and today's precarious employees dwarfs the gap between slaves and slave-owners, or between serfs and landlords.

So, does exploitation occur in a capitalist society like it did in previously existing social–economic formations? This society is comprised, on the one hand, of a majority who barely make ends meet, even while working hard, and on the other hand of a small number of people who are unfathomably wealthy — though they can't be working that much harder. People in the top 1% rake in about $5–$7 million a year, on average, while the average worker's income is about $50,000 (the median is $31,000, so you can see that many make far less).

That's just income; what about wealth? When it comes to assets, One-Percenters hold over $8 million; about 70 times more than the average person. And the top one percent of the One Percent, the 0.01%, take home over $25 million in income per year, well over 500 times the average.

But if the question is whether a capitalist society has such *exploitation* as exists in slave society or feudalism, it's hard to answer. We clearly find a structure of exploitation in a slave society or a feudal society. That's because most of the wealth owned by slave-owners or feudal lords is taken from the product of slaves or serfs' work. But if you take a close look at the relationship between workers and capitalists in a capitalist society, you can't be quite sure if exploitation exists or not. Apparently, workers work at their work places and collect their weekly or monthly salaries as the price of their labor. If their salary is too small, they may complain, wondering, "Is this my value?"

Is a capitalist society really exploitative?

Lecturer: OK, now keep that question in mind until our next class. Next week is going to be important — I'm going to demonstrate in numbers whether capitalist societies are as exploitative as a slave society or feudal society.

Student A: Oh, can that be proven in numbers? It would be pretty great if someone could perform such a calculation!

Lecturer: Yes, I can prove it in numbers. That's why it's all the more shocking. Of course, people may have different opinions on whether Marx's calculation makes sense or not.

Student B: Now that I've been following your lectures, it's gotten a bit clearer what I should get from this course. As a matter of fact, I'm really curious. *Does* exploitation exist in a capitalist society? If yes, it means that the enormous wealth owned by capitalists is actually what they've taken from the outcome of workers' hard work. That's not something to brush off.

Student C: I once heard in the news about workers at a clothing company who created a labor union and were fighting for their rights. One worker said that while she made several pieces of luxury clothing a month, she couldn't buy one for herself even with several months' pay checks. When you stop to think about that, it does seem like something's wrong. The worker was making several pieces of those clothes.... Since then, I've understood that capitalist societies clearly exploit workers as well.

Student D: In Economics classes, we learn that the wages for workers too are decided on the principle of the balance between demand and supply in the labor market. So, your course is rather confusing to me. I wonder what's next!

Points to Ponder

- What are the criteria by which we distinguish different types of societies?
- What is exploitation and how does it show up in different societies?
- Is a capitalist society exploitative?

LECTURE 2 — CAPITALISM TURNS EVERYTHING INTO A
COMMODITY

Lecturer: In our first lecture, we discussed why we should study *Das Kapital*. As the book is pretty tough, if you don't have a clear goal, you're likely to get tired pretty quickly. I've seen it with people I know. Any of you feeling like that?

Student A: I'm a Civil Engineering major. I know people call Engineering majors uncool nerds, so my friends and I organized a reading club with the idea of learning more about culture and the social sciences. Our first reading of *Das Kapital* was last semester, and we had fifteen eager members. But our following sessions had far fewer participants, until the club fizzled out.

Student B: I read the book on my own, and from the outset, it was really overwhelming. It was a long series of commodities and value, which I found pretty dull and totally beyond my understanding .... Now, the book just sits on my bookshelf.

Lecturer: You're referring to "Commodities and Money", right? In *Das Kapital*, earlier parts serve as the basis for what comes later, so if you fail to understand things gradually, as if you were building a tower, and skip things instead, you'll hit the wall and give up. Just as you can't properly understand Newtonian dynamics unless you solidly understand concepts such as mass, velocity, and force. And in this class, we're going to deal with 'Commodities and Money'.

Student C: Oh, we should batten down the hatches and hand on for the ride!

Lecturer: Well, that makes me sound like I'm giving you guys cold feet. If you look at the text of *Das Kapital*, 'Commodities and Money', it includes many abstract concepts as well as lengthy explanations. Since you feel like the author has his head in the clouds, you don't quite get at what it's trying to say. Today, you guys can take it easy, because I'm going to give a summary of its essentials.

Students: Thanks!

Start with Commodities in studying capitalism

Lecturer: Then, let's start. The main characteristic of capitalism is the capitalist-worker relationship, that is, the capitalist relations of production. Now, you remember.

In our first lecture, we asked ourselves if exploitation would exist in a capitalist society as in a slave society or a feudal society. To see whether a capitalist society is based on exploitation or not, how should we start our analysis?

In a slave society or a feudal society, exploitation of the ruled by the ruling class is conspicuous. Slave-owners or lords of the manors accumulated their wealth by using their power derived from their social status. In a capitalist society, however, workers and capitalists are legally equal. Unlike slaves or serfs, workers also enjoy the freedom to seek jobs. They don't have to be bound to specific companies and work there only. Workers can freely sell their labor power to whichever they like, Samsung, LG, Hyundai, SK, or Kookmin Bank. Problem is, the companies don't have to buy it.

Students: Hahaha, that's right!

Lecturer: The capitalist relations of production establish a bilateral contract by which workers supply their labor power to capitalists and capitalists in return pay wages to workers. It is a contract that is created with the free will of contracting parties. If unemployed young people feel bad when they fail to get a job, that's their free choice — from the perspective of mainstream economics. The underlying understanding is that they could settle for a passable employer, but those youths have chosen to remain jobless because they think they can afford to take their time and wait for a "perfect" job.

Anyway, the economic activities generated by the contract between capitalists and workers give rise to enormous gaps between rich and poor. Hired by capitalists, employees work in the factory to make various things such as computers, cell phones, or even bread, to print T-shirts and assemble cars. Capitalists make money by selling them in the market. And they pay wages to workers and take the remainder as their own.

Usually, the profits that capitalists earn are much more than the wages received by workers. That doesn't mean that capitalists pocket wages that were promised to workers. In a capitalist society, this process repeats endlessly in daily life.

So, where can we find a clue about the secrets related to exploitation?

Student A: As you began the class today, you briefly mentioned that the introduction of *Das Kapital* discusses commodities and money. I wonder if Marx began his book that way, perhaps, because a clue lies in 'commodities'. Made at the factory by workers, computers, cell phones, bread, T-shirts and cars are all commodities. Workers make them not to use them but to sell them. In a capitalist society, everyone is hell-bent on making money and people have to sell things to earn money. Workers sell their ability to work, capitalists sell things made by their companies, and banks sell loans. So, my wild guess is that maybe commodities serve as a clue.

Lecturer: Good hunch! Actually, the heart of today's lecture is how commodities form their value. You must have read my book — ☺ ?

Student A: I'm repeating the course, so I *did* read it last semester, haha ....

Lecturer: Oh, you did! Well, you're right, things that people make solely in order to sell them in the market (such as computers, cell phones, bread, T-shirts and cars) are called *commodities*. So, given that they're sold in the market, commodities are traded for *money*.

In a capitalist society, such activities occur all over the place. That's because most of the goods and services we need for our livelihood are supplied to the market as commodities to be traded for money. In addition, raw materials and machines required for operating factories are commodities purchased from the market. Raw materials and machines must be produced by someone for sale. Even the service of cutting your hair and styling it has to be purchased with money.

Most of the goods produced in a capitalist society are commodities. They're designed to be sold; they aren't made to be used by the makers. One characteristic of a capitalist society is that nearly all the imaginable goods or services are made into commodities.

When I was young, water was the last thing that people would pay for. Today, however, we're quite used to buying drinking water. Moreover, knowledge in all its forms that humankind has developed is now created and made available for sale as patents. Humans are commodities, too. People who seek jobs through a temp agency and anyone who applies for company jobs gussy up their labor power as commodities and ask companies to choose them. In secret markets, human organs such as kidney or eyeballs are sold. So, is there anything that capitalism cannot make into a commodity?

Capitalism turns everything into a commodity

Student A: It makes sense. I wonder if there's anything that capitalism can't make into a commodity. With air pollution getting so bad, I'm worried if air will be made into a commodity later. If so, we won't be able to breathe without money?

Lecturer: I heard that in China, where they suffer from severe air pollution, 'Canadian-made air' is a big seller. What great power capitalism has to turn everything into a commodity...!

When everything becomes a commodity, it's important *whether specific commodity may be purchased.* If you have a lot of money, you can purchase a large quantity of commodities, but if you have no money, you can't get your desired amount of the commodities. In short, a gap between rich and poor suggests that a small number of people have the exclusive right to buy and use a great number of commodities available in a society. As the first step in identifying the cause, Karl Marx analyzed commodities. It was an inevitable start in correctly understanding the capitalist society that turns everything into a commodity.

Student B: Professor, I've found one thing that cannot be a commodity. The human heart isn't for sale, is it?

Student C: I guess the human heart too can be bought. They say, follow the money, find the heart. When we see a rich young man winning a beautiful young lady's heart, shouldn't we admit that the human heart can be traded for money?

Lecturer: Haha, now if hearts can be bought with money, I'm not sure whether it's comedy or tragedy. Anyway, shall we start our full-blown analysis of commodities?

Marx said that a commodity has two different values. One is *use value* and the other is *exchange value*. Isn't it a bit weird? These are important concepts, so please write down on your notebook *use value and exchange value.*

Use value vs Exchange value

When a commodity has use value and exchange value, we can put it this way, too. Without use value and exchange value, goods or services aren't commodities. What do use value and exchange value mean?

First of all, if a commodity has *use value*, that means that it is *useful*. The use value of a computer lies in its fast calculation. The use value of a cell phone is that it enables a user to get in touch with someone far away immediately. I'm a great wine lover. The use value of wine is the distinctive flavor and fragrance that is quite distinct from any other.

If a commodity has no use value, in other words, if it's totally useless, it never sells in the market. It simply doesn't qualify as a commodity. My throat is in bad shape from frequent lectures I'm giving lately. So, I get a lot of mucus. And if I gather this and try to sell it, it will never sell, right?

Student E: It won't! Mucus is useless, Professor. But, if they're useful, any goods or services can be commodities?

Lecturer: Not necessarily. Earlier, I mentioned Canadian-made air is sold in China, but that looks like an exceptional case. In general, people don't sell or buy air. Still, air has great use value; that is, it is greatly useful. Without air, we would all lose our life in a few minutes. If it has such great use value, then why does air fail to be a commodity?

Student F: Professor, you said earlier today that commodities have use value and exchange value. Is it because air has only use value and doesn't have exchange value?

Lecturer: That's right. As you just said, air has use value and lacks exchange value. That's why — at least so far — air cannot be a commodity. Then, what attribute of a commodity does exchange value represent?

Let's focus on the term 'exchange'. Where does exchange of commodities mainly take place? It's the market. Whether it engages in barter or adopts money as its mediator, the market is a space-time construct where countless commodities are gathered for a complex trade-off. As Marx saw it, the pricing and exchange of commodities in the market essentially consisted in the trade-off of people's labor invested in making those different goods. For example, we can think of an exchange between a television and an MP3 player in the market. What it essentially means is a trade between the labor of the person who has made the television and that of the person who has made the MP3 player. So, it's a kind of trade-off. You exchange labor with some other person when commodities are traded.

Student G: In other words, when company workers use their salaries to buy products from a discount store, countless people are basically engaged in complex exchange of labor through the medium of money. It's my labor and some other person's labor being exchanged as commodities through the medium of money.

Lecturer: That's right. Exchange value as mentioned by Marx suggests that commodities have to be products of labor. When commodities are exchanged in the market, it means a trade-off of specific labor invested in making different products. In other words, things that aren't products of labor have no exchange value and thus cannot be commodities.

Student G: Oh, you mean, even though air is useful, it isn't a commodity because it isn't a product of labor. Now I see; that makes sense. No sane person would like to trade his or her product made with hard work for air which can be obtained with no effort.

Lecturer: Correct. But we can think of the opposite. There are things that cannot be commodities because they're useless, even if they're products of labor. Let's say that I've torn one of my books at home into pieces. Pieces of paper as such are clearly products of labor, but since they have lost their usefulness (use value) in conveying information and knowledge, they have lost their attribute as a commodity

To sum it up, commodities (whether goods or services) have two intrinsic qualities. One, they have a use value, that is, they are perceived as useful; and two, they have an exchange value, which has to do with the labor that goes into producing them.

How is the commodities exchange value decided?

Student G: That raises a question, Professor. How is the commodities exchange value decided in the market? For example, like ten television sets being of equal value to one car, or two computers traded for one copying machine. We usually call it *price*, right? Mainstream economics says that price is decided where supply and demand meet. Does Marx explain it in the same way?

Lecturer: I was just going to talk about *exchange value!* Why is it that one television is exchanged for fifty T-shirts instead of one T-shirt? Marx said that the quantitative ratio by which commodities are exchanged in the market is decided by the *socially necessary labor time* to produce the specific goods. And this is where his theory registers the biggest difference with the so-called mainstream economics. Let's say that it takes 150 labor hours to make one television whereas it takes 3 labor hours to make one T-shirt. To steer clear of any loss to either party, the goods should be exchanged in the following ratio.

1 television (150 labor hours) = 50 T-shirts
3 labor hours x 50 pieces = 150 labor hours

Student G just reminded us that mainstream economics states that prices are decided as the point at which supply and demand meet, right? Of course, the price is influenced by supply and demand. Marx knew that very well and *did* discuss it in *Das Kapital.* There is a difficulty in describing price as the point at which supply and demand meet, though. It cannot clearly explain why the price of a commodity is set at a specific level.

To be clear, when the price for an Equus sedan comes to around $100,000, why does a white board eraser cost $2? Even if there's a crushing oversupply of Equus sedans and nobody is buying, the car price wouldn't come anywhere close to $2. Or, even if the market suffers from severe shortages of white board erasers and there's an explosive demand, the price wouldn't be anywhere close to $100,000. You can say that an Equus is costly as it includes a lot more parts than an eraser. But, if someone asks how the prices of the different components of the Equus were arrived at, no one would be able to give a clear answer.

While price is influenced by shifts in supply and demand, it usually stays around a specific break-even point. Still, supply and demand can't clearly explain why such a break-even point occurs and how it forms.

Das Kapital describes how a break-even point for commodities exchange is formed. What decides the commodities exchange value is the labor time socially necessary to produce specific goods. As I said earlier, let's say that it takes 150 labor hours to make one television while it takes 3 labor hours to make one T-shirt. Suppose three television-making workers and three T-shirt-making workers work a total of 150 labor hours each, how many television sets and T-shirts will be produced? As each worker makes one television set, a total of three sets will be produced. Likewise, with each worker making 50 T-shirts in total 150 labor hours, 3 workers will make 150 T-shirts. After all, the market will receive 3 television sets and 150 T-shirts. And the break-even point will have one television set exchanged for 50 T-shirts.

Here, let's assume that the television-making workers increase to 6 persons. Then, the market will have 6 television sets, and with the same 3 workers working for T-shirt, 150 T-shirts will be made available as before. With changes applied, 1 television may be exchanged for 25 T-shirts for a while. But such a situation cannot persist. If one television set (requiring 150 labor hours) is exchanged for 25 T-shirts (requiring total 75 labor hours), the former would obviously be short-changed. The person's two labor hours is thus exchanged for the other person's one labor hour. When several television makers suffer losses and go out of business, the supply of television sets decreases to a break-even point.

Marx said that the socially necessary labor time is the element that essentially determines the break-even point for the commodities exchange value. And this is Marx's *labor theory of value*. It means that *the exchange value of a commodity is created by labor*.

Marx's labor theory of value

Student G: So, human labor gives value to commodities. Sure, I doubt that anything could be made without labor. It sounds logical. But, when we could just call it *labor time*, why use a cumbersome expression like *socially necessary labor time*?

Lecturer: There's an important reason. Let me take an example to explain it. Suppose that I'm a rookie mechanic that makes television sets. While workers spend average 150 labor hours to make a television set, it takes me 300 hours since I'm less skilled. Now, I'm taking the TV to the market, and if I've spent twice as many hours as others would spend to make one TV and I try to sell it at twice the price, what's going to happen? It won't sell. I wouldn't be able to sell it at anything more than the market price. 300 labor hours of a less skillful worker has been socially evaluated as 150 labor hours.

On the other hand, let's suppose that I'm a skillful worker with quick hands and I made a television in just 75 hours that would otherwise take average 150 hours. Still, my TV wouldn't sell at half price in the market, right? Mine, too, will sell at the existing market price. My skillful 75 hours are socially recognized as the equivalent of 150 labor hours.

Socially necessary labor time refers to how much time is needed, assuming a society's average skillfulness, average work intensity, and average productive forces. So, when we talk about how much time it takes to make a product, we need to distinguish *labor time* and *time*. Labor time refers to the time it takes when we assume average work intensity, skillfulness, and productive forces.

Student G: OK, so that's why they call it socially necessary labor time. Well, even if I put in two straight all-nighters to make one ballpoint pen, it wouldn't have the value of 48 labor hours.

Lecturer: To sum up, exchange value, by which commodities are exchanged in the marketplace (the underlying basis, the metrics, of the commodities exchange), is based on the labor time socially needed to make those products. For example, building a house takes a lot of socially necessary labor time. On the other hand, making one ballpoint pen takes far less socially necessary labor time. You just need to use your common sense to see that normally, more expensive goods are those that take more time to produce and cheaper goods are those that take less time to make.

Keep in mind what exchange value means. It is a core concept that will shed light on the exploitative structure of capitalism.

Student G: "Commodities have use value and exchange value. While use value indicates that a commodity is useful, exchange value suggests that a commodity must be a product of labor. And the commodities exchange value is decided by the labor time socially needed to produce specific goods." A summary like this makes it easier to understand the whole rigmarole.

Student H: But I have one question. While it sounds somewhat plausible that the commodities exchange value is decided by the labor time socially needed to produce specific goods, the actual execution has yet to be verified, right? And they don't measure the actual time it takes to make a product and compare different measurements in the market, do they? I guess that your lecture will get its logic from this labor theory of value. That's why I have to make sure I understand it more precisely.

Working time, the core element that determines exchange ratio

Lecturer: That's a sharp question. As you said, the labor theory of value makes the basis for what follows next. And that's why scholars who criticize the theory of *Das Kapital* focus their attacks on the labor theory of value. You may have asked your question just casually, but it is a very controversial and tough topic.

Let me use an analogy. High school physics presents the problem of calculating the time it takes for an object at a specified height to take a free fall and reach the ground. Remember?

Student H: I don't remember much from Physics...

Lecturer: OK, well, the time which it takes for an object to take a free fall and reach the ground is influenced by several factors. Such as wind, air resistance, air density, and even the distance from the Earth to the moon.,, All these factors influence the time it takes for an object to reach the ground. In solving physics problems, you don't consider all these factors. You just calculate by considering the physical quantity of gravitational acceleration. Then, is it a wrong theory that includes only gravitational acceleration in calculation and doesn't consider other elements?

Student H: I'm afraid we can't say it's absolutely wrong. Because the crucial physical quantity that determines the time it takes for an object to fall freely is gravitational acceleration, which alone can come up with approximate values. And it can be applied in actual situations.

Lecturer: That's right. You can understand the meaning of the labor theory of value in a similar way. In the market, the commodities exchange value is influenced by various factors including supply-demand gaps and brand recognition. However, Marx considered labor time as the crucial factor that determines the commodities exchange ratio. Some of you guys may remain skeptical.

For now, let's check what theories Marx advances, on the basis of the labor theory of value.

Student H: I never expected that physics would come up in a lecture on *Das Kapital*. Haha. Now I understand the context of your words.

Lecturer: If my analogy was too much of a stretch for you, never mind. What we discussed today is crucial, as it's the basis for the later development of capital. And while you may forget about all the other things, I want you to remember that the commodities exchange value is decided by the labor time socially needed to produce specific goods.

So far, we've briefly surveyed how Marx described the value of commodities in *Das Kapital*. This conversation may have sounded rather strange. But as they say, "No pain, no gain" and "There is no easy road to learning". Step by step, you'll reach your goal. I'll see you next time.

Points to Ponder

- What is a commodity?
- Why did Marx start his study of capitalism with an analysis of commodities?
- What are use value and exchange value?
- How is the commodities exchange value determined?
- What is the meaning of socially necessary labor time?

LECTURE 3 — MONEY HAS TURNED INTO CAPITAL

Lecturer: Finally, we're going full steam into the core part of Marx's *Das Kapital*. The heart of today's lecture is to understand the difference between *money* and *capital*. If you get a solid understanding of this, you'll have grasped the essence.

Student A: Professor, capital refers to a large amount of money, doesn't it? While you won't refer to 10 cents as capital, you could easily call $1,000,000 as such.

Lecturer: We get that sense when we use the word capital in our daily life. In *Das Kapital*, however, the term of capital is used differently. It is crucial to clearly understand the difference between money and capital. Look carefully at what I'm writing on the blackboard!

The birth of money is inevitable

C–M–C

Here, C is the first letter of *commodity* and M is the first letter of *money*. These two abbreviations will be used frequently in this discussion.

C (commodity)–M (money)–C (commodity)

So, what on earth does this formula represent? Suppose that I'm a maker and seller of clothes. I meet a person who needs clothes in the market and when a deal is cut, I deliver clothes and receive money for them. And I go to a wine store to buy wine with the money. At the wine store, I choose wine and pay the employee to conclude a transaction. I can describe this series of transactions with the formula I mentioned earlier.

C (clothes)–M (money)–C (wine)

Clothes and wine are commodities and are marked as C, while money is marked as M. In fact, the formula of C–M–C is a simple description of the series of transactions.

Now, let's talk about money for a moment. Let's assume that all currencies are gone. Then, how would we make our transactions?

Student B: Isn't it perhaps barter? You were just talking about making money by selling clothes and buying wine with the money. If there were no such thing as money, people would take their clothes to a wine store and trade them for wine.

Lecturer: However, if the wine store tells you that it doesn't need the clothes, what would you do? We'd have to ask them what they do need. If they tell you that they want *Phellinus linteus*, a mushroom variety, you'll have to go and ask a store that sells *Phellinus linteus*. "I want wine, but they didn't accept clothes, so I asked what they wanted, and heard that they needed *Phellinus linteus*. And I'm here. Please give me *Phellinus linteus*." But, what if the *Phellinus linteus* store says that they don't want clothes, either?

Student C: I'm afraid you won't be able to make a deal that way.

What is money and what is capital?

Lecturer: I think you see the point. Advancement of the division of work in a society and diversification of goods inevitably lead to the rise of money. Today, the word "money" brings to mind bills and coins that serve only as currencies. But history shows us many cases in which, out of countless goods traded, one is selected and serves as a currency. For example, goods such as gold, silver, or silk served as currencies.

With the adoption of money, business transactions became easier. You sell clothes at the market and buy wine from a wine store with the money. If gold is used as a currency, transactions will proceed as shown in the formula below.

C (1 piece of clothes)–M (10 grams of gold)–C (2 bottles of wine)

"C (1 piece of clothing)–M (10 grams of gold)" shows the process in which clothes are turned into money. And "M (10 grams of gold)–C (2 bottles of wine)" describes the process in which the same money is exchanged for wine. These two processes occur in succession to make a single formula. Once gold is used as a currency, the value of other goods can be described in terms of gold as follows.

1 television set = 50 grams of gold
1 jumper = 10 grams of gold
1 car = 5 kilograms of gold
1 bottle of wine = 5 grams of gold

It is because of its special property that gold, out of so many goods, has come to serve as a currency. First of all, a small quantity can represent a great value. Just imagine using cotton as a currency. To buy a house, several truckloads of cotton wouldn't be enough. It should be really inconvenient.

Moreover, gold can express various quantity values. Even when processed into different sizes, gold doesn't lose its use value. For purchasing cheap goods, you can pay with small pieces of gold, and for expensive goods, you can pay larger pieces. What if you use automobiles as currency? If you cut a vehicle in half, it will lose its use value, right? Now it's useless, and it has become something that is not a commodity. Besides gold, we have silver, silk and other goods that share the critical property and can serve as currencies.

Student C: I understand that historically, currencies originated from goods. However, the bills and coins we use now don't serve as commodities like gold, silver, and silk, but are used solely as currencies. The exchange value of the paper a $100 bill is printed on isn't $100.

Lecturer: That's right. As currency developed, it became a pure sign for exchange value by shirking off cumbersome elements.

We've lingered over the emergence of currency and its functions. But remember that today's lecture is designed to help understand the difference between money and capital! Now, listen up. When money is used as a medium for exchange and transaction, as in the examples presented so far, it isn't called capital. It's just money. When it functions as capital, however, money operates this way:

M (money) – C (commodity) – M' (money)

This is called *the general formula for capital*. When money served merely as a medium for transactions, it was described with the formula of C–M–C. The general formula for capital has M and C change places. Furthermore, M at the end has " ' " (prime) attached to it. What is this formula trying to express?

Let me give you an example. I make clothes for sale as a kind of cottage industry. One day, my clothes start selling like crazy. Thus, I make quite a lot of money. This seed money is M, which stands far left on the general formula for capital.

M (seed money) – C – M'

When your business is cruising along, you'd better get out of making clothes all by yourself, create a company and go into clothing production on a larger scale. So, I spend the seed money to rent an office, purchase raw materials and machines, and hire workers, thus creating a company. Now I'm going to work hard to run the business; what would the seed money turn into?

Student D: You've created a clothing company, so wouldn't it turn into clothes?

Lecturer: Right. C at the center of the general formula for capital indicates the clothes produced by the company.

M (seed money) – C (clothes) – M'

By selling clothes you've produced, you make money. And M' at the right end of the formula refers to the earned money, that is, sales price.

M (seed money) – C (clothes) – M' (sales price)

At first glance, it looks like a waste of breath. It's about exchanging money for clothes and exchanging clothes for money. Wouldn't it be easier just to hold onto the money?

Student D: Well, but you get more money than you had at the outset.

Lecturer: Right. If the clothes sell well, profits are generated to increase the money. The sign " ' " in M' (as seen in the general formula for capital) is a mark that indicates an increase of money.

M–C–M' (= M+m)
m is for an amount of money added to the initial volume

If your money grows, won't you feel great? With more money, you make and sell more clothes, and the process repeats to let the money keep growing. And this can be expressed in the formula.

M–C–M'–C'–M''–C''–M'''–C'''–M''''...

The increasing number of " ' " right next to M suggests the continuous growth of money. When money kicks into its own growth and becomes dynamic like this, we say that the money has become *capital*.

Where does profit come from?

Lecturer: With the formula of C–M–C, in which money just serves as a medium of transaction, no more changes are registered once wine is purchased. On the contrary, if money starts to function as capital, the process of M–C–M' doesn't stop but continues. A capitalist who has increased $100,000 to $150,000 now uses his head to increase $150,000 to $300,000. The desire to endlessly pursue profits now serves as the propelling power that keeps M–C–M' in circulation. When money as a means of transaction becomes capital, money upgrades from *a means* to *an end*.

Student A: So, when money enters a process of endless self-multiplication, it is called capital. That's one lucid way to distinguish money from capital. But, how is it that money grows in size? You said that it grows with profit, but where does profit come from?

Lecturer: Actually, *where profit comes from* is the very heart of *Das Kapital*.

First of all, let me digress into a personal story. When I was young, I thought that making money, that is, making profits, derived from the act of getting goods cheap and selling them to others at higher prices. And I had a reason to believe so. At that time, I would read "factory price of 6 cents" on the packaging for candy that I bought for 10 cents. I found that confusing, so I asked my mother what it meant, and she explained that the shop owner lady was buying the stuff from the factory for 6 cents and selling it to me for 10 cents. When I heard that, I was as shocked as a kid could be. As a child, I thought that the shop lady was playing fast and loose with us kids. It's understandable, as I would have felt betrayed if a classmate who bought an eraser for 5 cents and sold it to me for 10 cents.

And as I gradually became aware of how life works, I came to think perhaps the essence of money making lay in the act of buying things cheap and selling them at a higher price. If you look at manufacturing, people add a little more money for profit on top of the costs for acquiring raw materials and machines and hiring workers before they sell their products. Thus, I was bound to believe that money-making was essentially a commercial transaction in which one gets goods cheap and selling them for more.

Reading Marx's *Das Kapital*, however, I came to see one important fact. It was that in essence *a pure form of profit* cannot occur merely from commercial transaction pure and simple, I mean, the act of getting goods cheap and selling them for more.

Student B: Uh oh. I still believe that profit's created by getting goods at a low price and selling them for more. So, how come you assert that profit doesn't come from such commercial transactions? I don't understand.

Lecturer: I understand your skepticism. My explanation will help your understanding. Let me write down the general formula for capital once again.

M ($1,000) – C (computer) – M' ($1,200)

I can explain the formula like this. Let's say that I have $1,000 on me and that I buy a $1,000 computer with the money before I sell it to a student here for $1,200. Then, I've made $200, right?

Student B: Yes.

Lecturer: To make $200 through such a simple commercial transaction, you need to have a business partner. A deal can be concluded only if you buy the $1,000 computer from me for $1,200, right?

Student B: Of course.

Lecturer: When the transaction is viewed from the general perspective of this classroom, where you and I are together, what do we see? I've gained $200, but you paid $1,200 for the $1,000 computer, meaning that you've lost the value of $200. It's +$200 for one party and –$200 for the other, so the sum total is 0. So, for the entire class, is there any *newly created value* or *pure profit*?

Student B: None ... after all, it's zero sum. Hmmm ... ah, you mean, in a commercial transaction that trades things owned by two parties, *redistribution of wealth* takes place between the parties involved but there's no pure form of profit.

The circulation process cannot create value

Lecturer: Exactly. Now, it's time to explain the expression, *circulation process*. In general, the circulation process is the process by which goods are exchanged (whether through barter or mediated by currency). Aside from the circulation process, we have the *production process*. The production process refers to the process by which workers make products, using raw materials, machines and so on. In a nutshell, the production process is about making products, and the circulation process is about getting commodities exchanged in the market for some other commodities.

As I mentioned it earlier, no pure form of profit can come from the circulation process in which things are merely exchanged. Let's say that next year people will only exchange things from their homes. Stuff from my home will be moved to some other person's home, while stuff from that person's home will come to my place. While the ownership and location of the property may change, there won't be any new value created. Similarly, when farmers don't grow crops, they can't get new crops, and when construction workers don't work, there won't be new buildings.

And for both the country's economy and world economy, GDP grows annually at a specified rate. People quote a certain percentage as the average rate of profit for companies or industries. Each year, new stuff comes out and more goods appear. If this doesn't happen through the circulation process, where else is it happening?

Student C: Aren't things be made at factories, of course? They should come from the production area. People have to work to come up with something new. The mere act of exchanging can't create new value.

Lecturer: Correct. To create new value, people have to work to make new goods. Marx defined the exchange value of commodities as the labor time socially necessary to make the specific goods. From that standpoint, the new exchange value wouldn't be created without human labor. After all, we come to the conclusion that new value must be created not through the distribution process but through the production process.

Student C: So, for a close look at cases in which money functions as capital, we should analyze what happens in production process.

Lecturer: Sure. In our next lecture, we'll conduct a specific analysis of the production process. In the process, we'll be able to figure out what causes the severe gap between rich and poor in a capitalist society. Numbers will show whether exploitation exists or not.

Student D: That's fantastic! I look forward to it.

Lecturer: Oh, before I wrap up today's lecture, there's one thing I have to address. Some of those students who attended the class on distribution process asked if those who work in distribution are doing a valueless job. Actually, this question appears in Volume 2 of *Das Kapital*. I haven't mentioned the question so far, however, since it would be inappropriate to get into that in a beginner-level lecture. Still, I have questions like that, so I'll give a brief explanation.

In general, delivering products from producers to consumers is classified as the circulation process. In *Das Kapital*, however, transport is classified not as distribution but as part of the production process. That's not how we commonly understand it, is it? What Marx considered the circulation process is related exclusively to the process in which goods are exchanged.

For example, let's say that a planned economy is implemented in a communist society. Goods produced at factories go through warehouses and are delivered to consumers via distribution channels.

With this, we call it a day.

Points to Ponder:

- How did money develop?

- How different are capital and money?

- Explain the general formula for capital.

- Why is it that distribution process cannot create value?

LECTURE 4 — PROFIT COMES FROM TIME TAKEN AWAY
FROM WORKERS

Lecturer: In our previous lecture, we saw that we should take a look at the production process to figure out how profit arises in M–C–M'. Now, as we try to look into the production process, we change the general formula for capital like this.

M–C(LP, MP)–P–C'–M'

It's a bit longer now, isn't it? Don't worry. We can take time on this. The "C" in the middle of the formula M–C–M' has become "C(LP, MP)–P–C'". It shows a production process which wasn't available before the change.

M for money, which shows up for the first time in the formula, refers to the money that the capitalist has before he or she starts the business. For example, if I have $2,000,000 in startup capital for running a bread factory, that is M.

M–C(LP, MP) refers to the process in which the startup capital is spent to purchase goods required to produce bread. And coming in parentheses, LP and MP stand for labor power and means of production, respectively. To run a bread factory, you should hire workers with your startup capital, right? The workers' labor power, which is a commodities traded in labor market, is indicated as C(LP). And you should buy machines and raw materials, too? Goods like machines or raw materials are altogether referred to as means of production. So, it's marked as C(MP).

For example, M–C(LP, MP) refers to the process in which the seed money of $2,000,000 is spent to purchase goods required to produce bread. M for the money of $2,000,000 goes through an exchange process to transform into C for commodities such as labor power and means of production.

The value of labor power as a commodity

Student A: Professor, you said that labor power is also a commodity that is traded in labor market. In your previous lecture, you defined the exchange value of commodities as labor time socially necessary to produce them. Then, what does *exchange value of labor power* mean? Labor power after all refers to humans, and I can't quite clearly understand labor time that is socially necessary to produce humans.

Lecturer: That is a very good question. I was going to get there at an appropriate point, and you have asked the question. So, I'll have to mention it briefly. As you know, humans' ability to work, that is, labor power, doesn't come out of nothing. If workers are to work every day at a factory, they must eat food. They need places to sleep and they need clothes. They need recreation and refreshment. Also, they need to have and raise kids. From a capitalist's perspective, discontinuation of the work force would be pretty distressful, since there would be no workers available for factories. Workers handle all these issues by receiving wages from capitalists. After all, *wage* means the labor time socially necessary to maintain and reproduce their labor power. So, the wage received by workers represents the exchange value of their labor power.

Student A: I see. It takes various goods such as food and clothes to maintain and reproduce workers' labor power. Since workers pay for such goods with their wage, the value of their wage translates to the value of labor power maintained and reproduced, that is, that part of the commodity called labor power. Frankly, I have qualms about treating humans as commodities, but I can understand it.

How does capital grow?

Lecturer: I guess you got it right. Now, let's go back to where we were.

M–C(LP, MP) is immediately followed by C(LP, MP)–P, right? P is the first letter of production. C(LP, MP)–P refers to the process in which a capitalist uses MP for means of production and LP for labor power to start full-scale production of goods to sell in the market. It is a process in which the owner or CEO of a bread factory gathers his or her hired workers at the factory and produces bread with raw materials and bread machines.

P–C', which follows C(LP, MP)–P, represents P, the production process that makes C', the new product. P is for the production process that makes the bread, and C' is for bread produced. C'–M', which follows P–C', indicates the process in which M' for money is acquired by selling C' for commodity. Let's try a bread factory. It's about making M' for money by selling to the market C' for bread made in the production process. As you know, both C and M now have " ' " because the value has grown from M for startup capital. Profit has been created by selling bread to the market.

It starts with money, and going through the long process of M–C(LP, MP)–P–C'–M', has returned the initial type of money. And the change is the increased amount of money. The size has gotten bigger with profits. Thus, the capitalist has achieved his or her goal.

Now, let's take a closer look at what happens in production process. For simpler calculation, let's suppose that bread making requires only flour, a bread machine, and a worker. A worker supplies LP for labor power, while flour and the bread machine serve as MP for means of production. Now, for full-swing calculation, let's assume the following.

[Formula 1] 1kg of flour = 1 labor hour
    (amount of flour needed for 1 loaf of bread: 1kg)
[Formula 2] 1 bread machine = 10,000 labor hours
    (life of bread machine: production of 10,000 loaves of bread)

[Formula 3] Worker's daily pay (8 hours of work) = 1 loaf of bread
      (productivity: 1 worker produces 8 loaves of bread for 8 hours)

Student B: Well, the formulas give me headache. I'm not good at math. I was a math-hater in high school, and seeing those formulas, I'm stressed out.

Where does profit come from?

Lecturer: Don't worry. All our math will be simple addition, subtraction, multiplication, and division. Guess what's the toughest calculation for today? It's as difficult as 3 times 8. What's the answer?
Student C: 24, haha.
Lecturer: OK, let's do a little more. But, what you're going to hear today is something you've never heard anywhere. The conversation will be unfamiliar and the conclusion may perplex you. Still, keep your mind open and just follow the calculation.
So, let's check the meaning of these formulas.

[Formula 1] 1kg of flour = 1 labor hour

This formula says that 1kg has the exchange value of 1 labor hour. To be specific, it says that the labor time socially necessary to produce 1kg of flour is 1 labor hour. It takes time to sow wheat seeds, to pull weeds, to perform composting, to harvest crop, to thresh the wheat, and grind it into powder. If you divide the total of all these time lengths by the final output of flour, you get 1 hour per 1kg of flour.

[Formula 2] 1 bread machine = 10,000 labor hours
      (life of bread machine: productino of 10,000 loaves of bread)

This means that it takes 10,000 labor hours to make 1 bread machine. The added description is about the life of the bread machine, which is exhausted when 10,000 loaves of bread are produced. It means that the machine is no longer usable.

[Formula 3] Worker's daily pay (8 hours of work) = 1 loaf of bread

(productivity: 1 worker produces 8 loaves of bread for 8 hours)

This means that a worker works 8 hours a day and collects 1 loaf of bread as his or her daily pay. And productivity is mentioned. So, it means that a worker bakes 8 loaves by working 8 hours a day. That makes a loaf per hour.

Now, shall we calculate the exchange value for 1 loaf of bread produced at this factory? All we have to do is calculate the labor time socially necessary to bake one loaf, right? In order to make 1 loaf of bread, the worker kneads 1kg of flour and puts it in the bread machine. The worker operates the machine and gets 1 tasty loaf of bread in 1 hour. Some people may question where bread is made that way. But be advised that this is a situation simplified to make calculation easy. First of all, the whole of 1kg of flour goes into bread, right? Then, the exchange value for 1kg of flour is transferred intact to the baked bread.

[Formula 4] Exchange value of 1 loaf of bread = 1kg of flour +?

To make bread, you need not only flour but also a bread machine. Then, how does a bread machine contribute to creating the value of bread? While the used amount of flour should be reflected in calculation, bread baking doesn't consume a specific quantity of a bread machine as it does with flour. The machine runs today and will run tomorrow, just like that.

You're not sure how to do the calculation? Considering the *useful life* of the machine can make calculation easy. [Formula 2] stated that the machine should last long enough to produce 10,000 loaves of bread; that gives you the machine's estimated "life". Thus the exchange value for 1 bread machine is 10,000 labor hours. After all, we can say that the 10,000 labor hours held in 1 bread machine have moved entirely to 10,000 loaves of bread. This should make it easier to calculate how much of the exchange value the machine has transferred to 1 loaf of bread:

10,000 labor hours, the exchange value for 1 bread machine, divided by 10,000 loaves of bread, comes to 1 labor hour.

That's right. Each time 1 bread machine produces 1 loaf of bread, 1 labor hour out of 10,000 labor hours held in the machine is transferred to bread. And its life is exhausted when it has produced 10,000 loaves. We call this depreciation. Some of the questions on [Formula 4] have been answered. See the result as follows.

[Formula 5] Exchange value of 1 loaf of bread = 1kg of flour + depreciation of bread machine +?

We have seen how flour and bread machine contribute to creating the exchange value of bread. They have transferred their value to bread.

Now all we have left is worker's labor power, right? As I said on [Formula 3], the worker takes 1 hour to make 1 loaf of bread. This should complete the formula.

[Formula 6] Exchange value for 1 loaf of bread = 1kg of flour + depreciation of bread machine + worker's 1 labor hour

Now, let's calculate with specific numbers.

[Formula 7] Exchange value for 1 loaf of bread = 1 labor hour + 1 labor hour + 1 labor hour = 3 labor hours

As shown in [Formula 3], the worker works 8 hours a day to make 8 loaves of bread. So, the exchange value for 8 loaves will come from multiplying the value of 1 loaf by 8, right?

[Formula 8] Exchange value for 8 loaves of bread = 3 labor hours x 8 = 24 labor hours

The exchange value for 8 loaves of bread consists of 8kg of flour (8 labor hours), depreciation of bread machine (8 labor hours), and the worker's 8 labor hours. And this can be easily understood through the above calculation.

What were the elements that composed the exchange value

of bread? They were flour, the bread machine, and the worker's labor hours. And you can see that these three elements greatly differ in how their exchange value is transferred to bread. Flour and the bread machine transfer their exchange value intact to bread. For instance, 1 kg of flour transfers to the bread the exchange value of 1 labor hour, while 8kg of flour transfers to bread the exchange value of 8 labor hours. The bread machine also transfers to bread the exchange value that is commensurate to its depreciation. It transfers exactly its exchange value.

But the worker that the capitalist has hired for 1 loaf of bread essentially differs from means of production such as flour or the bread machine in how they transfer exchange value to bread. See [Formula 7]. The exchange value for 1 loaf of bread is 3 labor hours. But the worker who gets 1 loaf of bread for a day's work works 8 hours a day, way longer than 3 hours. This way, the worker creates in bread an exchange value which is tantamount to 8 labor hours. Thus, the worker has performed the *magic* that creates the exchange value of 8 labor hours, way longer than 3 labor hours, the exchange value for 1 loaf of bread.

At last, we have come close to an important clue that can show where profit originates in a capitalist society. To calculate this precisely, let's assume the following.

[Formula 9] 1 labor hour = $10

The formula shows that the amount of money $10 represents the exchange value for 1 labor hour. For example, a head phone worth $100 implies that the labor time socially necessary to make it is 10 labor hours. Back to the formula.

M–C(LP, MP)–P–C'–M'

I've given a lengthy description of the bread making process, which falls into P (production process) in the above formula. The worker worked 8 hours a day to make 8 loaves of bread. And it is represented by P–C' in the above formula. While P indicates the bread-making process, C' refers to bread, the commodity created through production process. The exchange value for the 8 loaves of bread which the worker made in one day is 24 labor hours, as may be seen from the result of [Formula 8].

Now, all the capitalist has to do is get money by selling to the market the bread made available by the production process. This is represented by C'–M' process. If we apply the hypothesis of [Formula 9], 8 loaves of bread are sold to get $240 in currency. For the exchange value for 8 loaves is 24 labor hours. And the result of the calculation is as follows.

M–C(LP, MP)–P–C'–M'
    C': 8 loaves of bread = 24 labor hours
    M': $240

Supposing that one worker produces 8 loaves of bread a day, I'll calculate and fill the rest of the formula.

M–C(LP, MP) shows how startup capital purchases MP for means of production and LP for labor power. And C(LP, MP) must represent the exchange value of 1 worker's daily pay and the means of production required to make 8 loaves of bread, right? 1 loaf of bread is paid to the one worker for his or her daily work. The exchange value for 1 loaf of bread is 3 labor hours and, given the hypothesis of [Formula 9], translates to a monetary value of $30. 8kg of flour (8 labor hours) and the amount of depreciation for the bread machine (8 labor hours) in combination makes 16 labor hours, while given the hypothesis of [Formula 9], it is $160. Therefore, startup capital M needed in the process of M–C(LP, MP) is $190 because $30+$160 = $190. Reflected in the formula, it comes as follows.

M–C(LP, MP)–P–C'–M'
    M: $190
    C(LP, MP): flour (8) + machine depreciation (8) + labor power (3) = 19 labor hours
    C': 8 loaves of bread = 24 labor hours
    M': $240

C(LP, MP)–P describes the process in which acquired means of production and labor power are used to make bread. P–C' shows how P, the production process, comes up with C', the 8 loaves of bread. As calculated with [Formula 8], the exchange value for 8 loaves of bread is 24 labor hours. C'–M' refers to the process in which bread is sold in the market to retrieve money. As calculated earlier, they get $240.

As you see, the amount, which was $190 at the start, is now $240. As much as $50 has increased. And this is the capitalist's profit. Where does this come from? Anyone?

Student A: Because flour and machines transfer their value intact to the bread during the production process, there's no way that new value is going to come out of it. So, profit can only come from labor power. The worker gets 1 loaf of bread for a day's work and works 8 hours a day. Subtract from those 8 hours the 3 labor hours that equal the value of 1 loaf of bread. You get 5 hours, which precisely matches $50 which the capitalist pockets.

Lecturer: Right! The worker gets 1 loaf of bread ($30) as his or her daily pay, but works 8 hours a day. If you subtract 3 labor hours for the bread the worker got, that leaves the value of 5 labor hours, worth $50. The capitalist's profit goes up when the worker works more than enough to cover the wage paid.

Student A: His analysis is pretty novel! I've never heard of such an argument before. In your first lecture, you said that the exploitative structure of a capitalist society could be demonstrated by numbers, which is this.

Provided 100 workers work in such working conditions at a bread factory, the capitalist collects a profit of $50 per worker. Multiply this by 100 persons, and the capitalist collects $5,000 each day. After all, the capitalist alone can become rich in this arrangement. 100 workers work 8 hours a day, 5 hours out of which they work for the capitalist.

Frankly, this is no different from the ancient slave society. Shocking.

Lecturer: Let's say that a big corporation hires 100,000 people. If the company can take an hour away from each employee, how many hours would it take from them all? That's 100,000 hours. If those people work 100,000 hours a day for me, how could I fail to become rich? Of course, assuming that the products made by the company sell. So yes, slave-owners take time away from slaves, feudal lords from serfs, and likewise, according to *Das Kapital*, in a capitalist society, a capitalist takes time from workers.

Surplus value and commodity value

Student A: I've never thought before that one could view capitalism from this perspective. I'm honestly pretty confused now.

Lecturer: I'm not done yet, so please bear with me. Here, I have to introduce to you new concepts of constant capital and variable capital.

The so-called means of production mentioned earlier, such as flour or a bread machine, gets its exchange value transferred intact to commodities. The capital used to purchase such means of production is called *constant capital*. From the first letter, it is labeled C. Don't confuse it with the C of commodity. The word *constant* implies transfer of unchanged value.

On the other hand, capital which is used to hire workers is called *variable capital*. The word *variable* is used here, because workers can create greater value than their wage measures. A worker who gets 1 loaf of bread (3 labor hours) as his or her daily pay creates an exchange value that amounts to 8 labor hours (by working 8 hours a day). And it is marked as V from the first letter of *variable*.

Now, I'm going to use the concepts of constant capital and variable capital to reconstruct the exchange value for 8 loaves of bread that the worker produced in a day. Constant capital C and variable capital V are as follows.

Constant capital C
= 8 labor hours (flour) + 8 labor hours (amount of depreciation of bread machine)
= 16 labor hours = $160

Variable capital V
= 3 labor hours (worker's daily pay) = $30

The capitalist's cost for purchasing constant capital C and variable capital V was the startup capital M, that is, $190. And the value of the eight loaves of bread that rolled out of the production line is formulated like this.

Exchange value of 8 loaves of bread

= 8kg of flour (8 labor hours) + machine depreciation (8 labor hours) + worker's 8-hour work (8 labor hours)
= 24 labor hours

Here, "8kg of flour (8 labor hours) + machine depreciation (8 labor hours)" refers to constant capital. It can be marked as C (16 labor hours).

Exchange value of 8 loaves of bread
= C(16 labor hours) + worker's 8-hour work (8 labor hours)
= 24 labor hours

How should we analyze the worker's 8-hour work? 3 hours out of the worker's 8-hour work is equal to the worker's daily pay of $30, right? These 3 hours can be marked as wage, that is, variable capital V. Then, the worker's 8-hour work is composed of V and 5 labor hours.

Exchange value of 8 loaves of bread
= C(16 labor hours) + V(3 labor hours) + 5 labor hours = 24 labor hours

Now, we have just 5 labor hours left. These 5 labor hours are the time that the capitalist took away from the worker, in other words, the time that the worker worked solely for the capitalist's profit. This is called *surplus labor*, and the exchange value created with surplus labor is called *surplus value*. Surplus value is marked as S. And it can be put into a formula as follows.

Exchange value of 8 loaves of bread
= C(16 labor hours) + V(3 labor hours) + S(5 labor hours) = 24 labor hours

In general, the value of a commodity is composed of the three elements of constant capital C, variable capital V, and surplus value S. This is important, so keep it in mind!

Exchange value of a commodity = C(constant capital)+V(variable capital)+S(surplus value)

A wage is the price of labor power

Student A: So, not only for the case of 8 loaves of bread just calculated, but all ordinary commodities, the exchange value is made up of these three factors. Until now, I thought that workers are paid for the exact amount of work that they do at worksites. Naturally, I thought that their wage is the price of their work, but Marx's analysis suggests that workers aren't being properly paid for their work.

Lecturer: You just made an important statement. According to *Das Kapital*, the wage isn't the price of work. The book clearly says that the wage isn't the price of work but *the price of labor power*. If the wage were the price of labor, a worker who makes 8 loaves of bread would receive not $30 but $80. In fact, however, the capitalist could not make any profit, paying such a wage. Lack of profit should ruin the business. In this condition, the capitalist system cannot function. In other words, *exploitation is necessary* in order for the capitalist system to function.

I just said that the wage is the price of labor power. The wage that a worker receives refers to the labor time that is socially necessary for the worker to maintain labor power.

Out of a bread-making worker's daily 8-hour work, only 3 hours counts as work for the worker and the remaining 5 hours are for the capitalist — this was proved by Marx with his concept of surplus value. Now, we know that a slave society and a feudal society are exploitative, because slave-owners and feudal lords accumulated their wealth by taking away the result of the work by slaves and serfs. Capitalists do the same; they take the surplus value produced by workers and make it their own. This is the concealed exploitative structure of the capitalist society.

In this sense, a *wage worker* is a modern-day slave. The exploitation is subtly covered up, so we don't know it when we live as *wage slaves*. It's such an odd system. The secret of the gap between rich and poor in a capitalist society lies in *time theft*.

Student A: That's depressing... Big corporate CEOs are bound to get hugely rich, because the surplus labor of the countless *wage slaves* they drive will fall into their lap. It's just so shocking that the wealth enjoyed by capitalists is actually workers' time taken away.

Student B: But, I have a question. Those figures designed to calculate exploitation, like 1kg of flour having the value of 1 labor hour, a bread machine is worth 10,000 labor hours, and a worker's daily pay is 1 loaf of bread. If these figures were changed, wouldn't we have a different outcome?

Lecturer: Of course, if you change the figures, the amount of stolen time will change, too. However, the exploitative structure, which is the essence, doesn't change. Marx basically thought that the value of a certain commodity was composed of the labor time necessary to produce it. We thus reach the conclusion that by taking part of the value by labeling it "profit," the capitalist, who doesn't work, can only steal the worker's time. When value comes solely from labor, a person who doesn't work can take value as profit only by taking away part of a worker's labor.

Student B: I see what you're saying. But, doesn't the capitalist also work at the company? And considering that the capitalist has invested his or her assets in the company at their own risk, shouldn't we take that into consideration?

Lecturer: Of course, capitalists work, too. However, if the managers they hire are doing what the capitalists should do, it doesn't mean that the managers can take all the profit. So, just because capitalists themselves are working doesn't mean that they can take the whole profit. To make a long story short, capitalists have the right to dispose of profit at their will because of their right to their companies, that is, their ownership.

Next, let's discuss the wealth of corporate owners from the perspective of *Das Kapital*. Their huge pools of capital have been accumulated since the companies' founding by taking away surplus value from countless workers. Even the big money, which capitalists say they earned because they took risks in investing, can be traced to its root and be shown as an outcome of past exploitation. Just as it's legal to drive slaves in a slave society, it is lawful in a capitalist society for an owner of capital to take all the profit.

Student B: Hmmm... that makes sense from the perspective of *Das Kapital*. It's a view that I never knew of, or thought of, before. If it wasn't persuasive, I would ignore it.... In fact, it's quite a plausible analysis.

Lecturer: You are puzzled, of course. It refutes what you've learned so far. As we go further, you're going to be in for more surprises. I'll say one more thing before I wrap it up for today.

We can put it in a different perspective that the worker's daily pay is $30 (3 labor hours). This should mean that I can maintain my current living standard by working just three hours a day. For the worker's portion would be just 3 hours out of 8 hours.

When folks talk about reducing working time, capitalists loudly claim that companies will go out of business, which is not true. In 19th century England, the Factory Act was introduced to shorten work hours, and the English capitalists were clamoring that companies would go belly up. We can shorten the working day. If work time is reduced without reducing wages, the capitalist gets less surplus labor. Capitalists doggedly oppose this reduction of working time because their gut tells them that profits will diminish.

This time, we have dug into profit. We have learned one important thing here: profit comes from *work taken away or exploited (surplus value)*. And this is the famous *theory of surplus value*. We have also seen that a wage is not the price of labor but the price of labor power. What we have discussed today is the core of Marx's *Das Kapital*

Points to Ponder

- How is the value of labor power decided?

- Where does the profit come from which arises from production?

- Let's tell the difference between constant capital and variable capital.

- What are the three factors that make up the exchange value of commodities?

- What's the social meaning of reduction of working time?

Lecture 5 — Why Do Companies Like It If You Work Late?

Lecturer: In the last class, we saw how profit is created in production. Do you remember the meaning of phrases like *surplus value*, *constant capital*, and *variable capital*? We used some math to show that capitalism is a form of society that runs with capitalists exploiting workers. And quite a few of our students were in shock.

Student A: I'm Economics major. In the Economics department, I've been studying mainstream economics such as micronomics and macronomics, and the theory of surplus value in your lecture pretty much confuses me. I feel like all my previous ideas are being overturned. It's such a hodgepodge now.

Student B: I've envied and respected those successful CEOs who have made a fortune. Honestly, I want to be a CEO like that, too. But, if Marx is right, capitalists can own such huge wealth only because they exploit workers. This, I find it pretty difficult to accept.

Lecturer: I understand your feelings. As a college student, I was totally shocked when I read and got the gist of *Das Kapital*. The more I studied it, however, the more I thought that its theory presented a more piercing analysis than anything else into the contradictions and conflicts embedded in capitalist society.

From this point forward, it gets more and more exciting.

Let's move on with the theory of surplus value.

Today, we're going to take a look at *production of absolute surplus value*. This phrase sounds a bit difficult. It refers to one of the actions that the capitalist takes to milk more profit out of workers.

Necessary labor and surplus labor

Lecturer: Today, we have one more person with us. His name is Jim. Jim is a bread baker. He gets a day's pay of 1 loaf of bread for 8 hours' work at a bread factory. Jim's 8 hours of work can be split into the two factors of necessary labor and surplus labor.

Jim's 8 labor hours = necessary labor (3 labor hours) + surplus labor (5 labor hours)

We have a strange phrase here, *necessary labor*. Let me explain. Let's say Jim gets one loaf of bread as his daily pay; we calculated its exchange value in our last lecture, didn't we? It's 3 labor hours, and $30 in money.

Jim's daily pay = exchange value of 1 loaf of bread = 3 labor hours = $30

Jim works eight hours a day, out of which three hours cover his day's pay. We call this portion *necessary labor*. The remaining five hours convert to the capitalist's profit; this portion of his work is called *surplus labor*.

Student A: In your last class, you called what a worker receives in wages *variable capital*, right? Now, you say *necessary labor*. How are they different?

Lecturer: Constant capital and variable capital are two different concepts that describe how value is transferred to products. Means of production, such as raw materials and machines, are transferred to commodities without changing their value. So, they are called constant capital. On the other hand, labor power transfers more value to commodities than workers' wages. Therefore, it is called variable capital. By the way, the concepts of necessary labor and surplus labor are meant to distinguish the *wage portion* and the *portion that converts to the capitalist's profit* out of a worker's daily working time.

Student A: OK. Now I clearly see how they differ. But, I'd be mad if my day's pay was just the three hours after working eight hours a day!

Lecturer: Jim isn't aware that out of eight hours he has worked, he was working only three hours for himself. Maybe, he thinks that his daily pay is for the eight hours he has worked. Because he never took this lecture on *Das Kapital*. Most workers who live in a capitalist society mistake their wage for the price of *labor*, when it is actually the price of *labor power*. Most wages are deferred payment, and so the monthly pay a worker receives for a month's work is quite likely to be considered as the price of one month of work.

Let's go back to where we were. Piece of Cake Bread Bakery, Jim's employer, lets Jim work just eight hours a day for a daily pay of $30 and sends him home on time. In contrast, Crushing Bread Bakery, where Russell works, expects ten hours' work a day for a daily pay of $30. Russell isn't happy about working late, but lacking any special skills and since he has to feed himself, he can't give up his job.

Let's see how daily working time is organized for the two men.

For Jim (Piece of Cake Bakery),
Daily 8 labor hours = necessary labor (3 labor hours) + surplus labor (5 labor hours)

For Russell (Crushing Bakery),
Daily 10 labor hours = necessary labor (3 labor hours) + surplus labor (7 labor hours)

Following our calculation so far, we assume that $10 is tantamount to 1 labor hour. Both Jim and Russell receive $30 for their daily pay, their necessary labor remains the same at 3 labor hours. As far as surplus labor goes, Jim puts in 5 labor hours and Russell puts in 7 labor hours. Crushing Bakery, Russell's employer, makes people work longer hours for the same daily pay, so his surplus labor adds up to 2 more hours.

You can easily see that when overtime work is required, as at Crushing Bakery, surplus labor increases and the capitalist can get more profit. Then, shall we calculate with formulas and see specifically how profit changes? We're bringing back the same formulas we used in our earlier lecture.

[Formula 1] 1kg of flour = 1 labor hour
(amount of flour needed for 1 loaf of bread: 1kg)
[Formula 2] 1 bread making machine = 10,000 labor hours
(life of bread machine: production of 10,000 loaves of bread)
[Formula 3] Worker's daily pay (8 hours of work) = 1 loaf of bread
(productivity: 1 worker produces 8 loaves of bread in 8 hours)

At Piece of Cake Bakery, Jim works 8 hours a day and makes 8 loaves of bread. Those 8 loaves of bread that Jim makes have the following value.

Exchange value of 8 loaves of bread
= 8kg of flour (8 labor hours) + depreciated amount of bread machine (8 labor hours) + worker's working time (8 labor hours) = 24 labor hours

Working for Crushing Bakery, Russell works 10 hours a day and makes 10 loaves of bread. Those 10 loaves of bread that Russell makes have the following value.

Exchange value of 10 loaves of bread
= 10kg of flour (10 labor hours) + depreciated amount of bread machine (10 labor hours) + worker's working time (10 labor hours) = 30 labor hours

These formulas are reconstructed into constant capital C, variable capital V, and surplus value S.

Exchange value of commodity
= C (constant capital) + V (variable capital) + S (surplus value)

Remember the formula? If you forgot, let's review it.

[For Jim]
[Formula 4] Exchange value of 8 loaves of bread
    = C(16 labor hours) + V(3 labor hours) + S(5 labor hours)
= 24 labor hours

In the value of the 8 loaves of bread that Jim made, constant capital C(16 labor hours) represents the exchange value of means of production, that is, flour and bread machinery. Variable capital V(3 labor hours) is for the wage portion. And surplus value S(5 labor hours) is the portion that the capitalist takes as profit.

[For Russell]
[Formula 5] Exchange value of 10 loaves of bread
    = C(20 labor hours) + V(3 labor hours) + S(7 labor hours)
= 30 labor hours

In the value of the 10 loaves of bread that Russell made, constant capital C(20 labor hours) represents the exchange value of means of production, that is, flour and bread machine. Again, variable capital V(3 labor hours) is for wage portion. And surplus value S(7 labor hours) is the portion that the capitalist takes as profit.

Students: Hmm....

Lecturer: Here, let me bring up the rate of profit.

Rate of profit
= Profit/(Invested capital) = S/(C+V)

The denominator has the sum of C(constant capital) + V(variable capital), and the numerator has S(surplus value). Why is it that C+V is in the denominator and S is in the numerator, and why is this formula called rate of profit? For the capitalist, constant capital C is facility investment used to buy means of production. For the capitalist, variable capital V is labor cost. Combining facility investment and labor cost, C+V is total *invested capital* for the capitalist. Surplus value S is the profit collected by the capitalist.

After all, the rate of profit is a concept that describes how much profit is created for invested capital. So, it must be very important to the capitalist, right?

Now, with the rate of profit formula, we calculate the rate of profit for Piece of Cake Bakery and Crushing Bakery. Let's say that Piece of Cake Bakery and Crushing Bakery both hire 100 employees each.

Piece of Cake Bakery has 100 employees and they work 8 hours a day, and each of the employees makes 8 loaves of bread a day. Thus the whole workforce is making 800 loaves of bread each day. And for the 800 loaves of bread, its exchange value may be reconstructed like this. We multiply [Formula 4], which is for Jim, by 100.

Exchange value of 800 loaves of bread
= C(1,600 labor hours) + V(300 labor hours) + S(500 labor hours) = 2,400 labor hours

With the figures for C, V, and S put into the rate of profit formula, we can get the following result. Sure, you get the same result even if you calculate on Jim alone, but more realistically, you assume 100 people are working.

Rate of profit for Piece of Cake Bakery = $S/(C+V)$ = 500/(1,600+300) = $5/19 \simeq 26.3\%$

※ Using the rate of profit defined by Marx himself, we can calculate the rate of profit for Piece of Cake Bakery as follows.

$S/(C+V)$ = 500/(1,000,000+800+300) = $5/10,011 \simeq 0.05\%$

In the denominator, 1,000,000 indicates the exchange value of 100 machines used by 100 workers (100 x 10,000 = 1,000,000), and 800 represents the exchange value of flour. In calculating the rate of profit, *capital* reflects the total value of a machine used in production. This is because invested capital in the denominator doesn't mean an amount of depreciation in a certain period of production but it refers to the total facilities. In this book, however, I'm putting into the rate of profit only 800 which is for the depreciation of the machine. In this calculation, the machine is considered expendable, just like flour. This is only for the convenience of calculation and smooth storytelling.

Crushing Bakery has 100 employees and they work 10 hours a day, so the whole workforce makes 1,000 loaves of bread each day. And for the 1,000 loaves of bread, its exchange value may be reconstructed like this. It's as easy as multiplying [Formula 5] by 100.

Exchange value of 1,000 loaves of bread
= C(2,000 labor hours) + V(300 labor hours) + S(700 labor hours) = 3,000 labor hours

The rate of profit is calculated like this.

Rate of profit for Crushing Bakery = $S/(C+V)$ = 700/ (2,000+300) = 7/23≈30.4%

Student A: Certainly, Crushing Bakery's rate of profit is 4% higher. Now I see why companies are dying to see their workers working late. It's because the longer workers work, the more profit the capitalist collects.

Producing absolute surplus value

Lecturer: This is what you can easily understand without going to the trouble of calculating the rate of profit. Undoubtedly, making workers work more for the same pay increases surplus labor, and the capitalist will have a larger share, that is, profit. Problem is, the tragedy doesn't end here.

Piece of Cake Bakery and Crushing Bakery are both bread makers, so they're rivals in the market. For workers, it's better to work at Piece of Cake Bakery than Crushing Bakery, right? Then, what is it like for a company that competes with another company?

As we have seen in the rate of profit calculation, Crushing Bakery creates more profit than Piece of Cake Bakery does by having their workers put in overtime. The company spends its extra profits in advertising, and research for improving their bread quality. Thus, they maintain their superiority over Piece of Cake Bakery and succeed in capturing the market. Defeated, Piece of Cake Bakery goes out of business. As baseball coaches say: "Nice guys finish last."

In a capitalist market economy, there's a cut-throat competition among companies. People aren't toting guns, but it's like a war zone. If you don't concentrate your resources to maximize your profits like Crushing Bakery does, you'll fall behind your competitors in market share. So, a dismal conclusion is that in the capitalist jungle, companies have to exploit their workers all the more.

It's not just to make more money and enjoy a cushy life that capitalists endlessly pursue profits and exploit workers. If they don't, they're going to be selected out of the capitalist competition. Just like that, the capitalist's personality reflects the limitless greed of capital.

Student A: That's scary! So, it's not that some capitalists with particularly bad personalities exploit workers. We have to conclude that capitalists have no choice but to milk workers just to survive the market competition. It's such an appalling reality. Mainstream economics never offers this explanation. The analysis exposes the predatory nature of capitalism.

Lecturer: Well, people say that economics is a dismal science. Anyway, now you understand what creating absolute surplus value is all about, don't you? It's particularly striking for Americans, who work far longer hours than even the Japanese, according to the International Labor Organization.

Student A: Well, is there such a thing as *producing relative surplus value*? Somehow, I guess there is the opposite concept of *absolute*.

Lecturer: Oh, haha, that's actually what's coming in our next lecture.

Points to Ponder:

- Explain necessary labor and surplus labor.

- Write the rate of profit formula and explain it.

- When wage remains the same and working time is extended, why does the capitalist's rate of profit increase?

- Why does the capitalist try to milk workers without end?

- Describe what it means to produce absolute surplus value.

LECTURE 6 — TECHNOLOGICAL DEVELOPMENT FURTHERS EXPLOITATION

Lecturer: Now, we know that in order to extract more surplus value, the source of his or her profit, and survive market competition with other capitalists, the capitalist will force long hours of work on workers. Producing absolute surplus value refers to the capitalist increasing the absolute amount of surplus value, in other words, the capitalist's portion, by extending the workers' working time.

Today, we're going to study the production of relative surplus value, as I said last time. You certainly remember Jim, who made a brief appearance as a bread-maker hired by Piece of Cake Bakery. He works 8 hours a day, with 3 labor hours as necessary labor and 5 labor hours as surplus labor.

[Jim's daily working time]
8 labor hours = necessary labor (3 labor hours) + surplus labor (5 labor hours)

The owner of Piece of Cake Bakery where Jim works was upset when he saw that Crushing Bakery was making more profit by having his people work 10 hours a day. To beat Crushing Bakery, the Piece of Cake Bakery extended the work day by 3 hours. With the daily wage remaining the same, of course. Jim's work day goes from 8 to 11 hours — with his day's pay unchanged. The necessary labor remains the same at 3 hours, while the surplus labor becomes 8 labor hours.

[Increased daily working time for Jim]
11 labor hours = necessary labor (3 labor hours) + surplus labor (8 labor hours)

With surplus labor increasing to 8 hours, Piece of Cake Bakery's profit increases by the same measure. This is called the creation of absolute surplus value.

Now the boss of Piece of Cake Bakery wanted to get the maximum possible surplus labor. "You guys are gonna work 30 hours a day!" he probably wanted to say. To his regret, however, there are only 24 hours in a day.

"OK, then I'll let them work 24 hours a day!"

Geez, you're going overboard! If they can't sleep, the workers will get sick and die.

"Then, they can sleep 8 hours and work 16 hours a day!"

Producing relative surplus value

Student A: Humans aren't beasts, how can they work like that? That's unrealistic. Is there such a capitalist on earth?

Lecturer: Unrealistic, eh? Truly inhumane and unhumanitarian. But such people really existed. When capitalism was budding, extreme work hours were pretty commonplace around the world. *Das Kapital* describes the exploitation of labor in England during the Industrial Revolution. There were cases that went beyond imagination, abuses that make me wonder if they were committed by humans.

A worker who ran away from work got branded, and children around the age of six were put into a factory and made to work 16 hours a day. Before Thomas Edison invented incandescent light bulbs, slaves could rest after sunset because it was too dark. Ironically enough, thanks to light bulbs, people could work overtime and even go through the night working.

Today, workers form labor unions to fight against such abuse, and laws and systems reflect their demands. This way, much of the severe exploitation of labor seen in the early days of the Industrial Revolution has been eliminated. In most countries, labor legislation puts a cap on daily working time, or stipulates payment of a surcharge for inevitably working overtime.

In today's world, production of absolute surplus value has hit the wall. Now it's difficult to force people to work long hours. Still, there's a way to increase surplus value. That's *production of relative surplus value*. How is this possible?

Piece of Cake Bakery's boss let out a sigh when he saw that labor laws limited daily working time to eight hours.

"Why does this world keep me from making money?"

If you were the boss of Piece of Cake Bakery, how would you increase surplus value if working time is limited to 8 hours as shown in this formula?

8 labor hours = necessary labor (3 labor hours) + surplus labor (5 labor hours)

Student B: If you can't increase working time, the only way must be by reducing the necessary labor time. If you reduce the 3 hours of necessary labor to 2 hours, the surplus labor increases from 5 hours to 6 hours.

Lecturer: That's right. So, to reduce the necessary labor time, what specific measures would the capitalist take?

Student B: Well, let's see. Necessary labor refers to the portion of a day's working time for which a worker is compensated with a day's pay, and reduced necessary labor time means, after all, a reduced wage for the worker. And it means that the capitalist reduces the wage. Because if he reduces the wage, the capitalist can get more for himself.

Lecturer: Theoretically, yes. But is it possible for a business to cut its employees' wages without a good reason? For example, let's say, necessary labor is reduced from 3 hours to 2.5 hours.

8 labor hours = necessary labor (2.5 labor hours) + surplus labor (5.5 labor hours)

This way, the Piece of Cake Bakery boss may say to himself, "Yee ha! how smart!" But reducing the necessary labor time to 2.5

hours means a day's pay is reduced from $30 to $25. And with their income so sharply cut, employees will be upset. So, unless the company is facing bankruptcy or a similar emergency, a unilateral pay cut isn't so realistic.

Student B: Then, is it unrealistic to produce surplus value by reducing necessary labor time?

Lecturer: Not really. It is actually possible in a way that you simply can't imagine. And learning what it is is the point of today's lecture.

Now, we're talking about a day's pay of $30, but we said 1 loaf of bread was the equivalent, right? I hope you remember that. The exchange value of 1 loaf of bread was 3 labor hours and it converted to $30 in money. Now, we put the daily pay at 1 loaf of bread again. This should make it easy to understand.

Previously, we set the exchange value of 1 loaf of bread at 3 labor hours. But what if the exchange value of 1 loaf of bread changes? The exchange value of 1 loaf of bread means the socially necessary labor time to produce 1 loaf of bread. Bread makers competing with one another may research, develop, and apply new bread-making technologies. With new technology and machines, what changes will bread production see?

Let me give a specific example. As done before, the exchange value of 1 loaf of bread is calculated like this.

Exchange value of 1 loaf of bread
= 1kg of flour (1 labor hour) + depreciated amount of bread machine (1 labor hour) + worker's labor time (1 labor hour) = 3 labor hours

Let's say they come up with a better bread machine. Most bread bakeries have installed the machine in their production lines. The exchange value of the new bread maker is the same 10,000 labor hours as of the old bread machine, and it works just as long — enough to produce 10,000 loaves of bread. The only difference is that with the new machine, a worker who puts in 8 hours a day can make 16 loaves of bread a day. That means 2 loaves of bread are produced each hour. With the old machine producing only 1 loaf of bread for 1 hour, it's a clear improvement in performance, isn't it? So, the exchange value of 16 loaves of bread that a worker produced in an 8-hour workday with the new machine can be calculated like this.

[Formula 1] Exchange value of 16 loaves of bread
= 16kg of flour (16 labor hours) + depreciated amount of bread machine (16 labor hours) + worker's 8-hour work (8 labor hours) = 40 labor hours

Producing 16 loaves of bread takes 16kg of flour, so an exchange value of 16 labor hours is transferred. Since the new bread machine has the same life as the old one, the depreciated amount transferred to 16 loaves of bread is 16 labor hours. As a worker has made 16 loaves of bread by working 8 hours, the exchange value that the worker has transferred to those 16 loaves of bread is 8 labor hours. The exchange value of 16 loaves of bread is therefore 40 labor hours.

The exchange value of 1 loaf of bread can be obtained easily by dividing the left-hand side and the right-hand side of [Formula 1].

[Formula 2] Exchange value of 1 loaf of bread
= 1kg of flour (1 labor hour) + depreciated amount of bread machine (1 labor hour) + worker's 0.5-hour work (0.5 labor hour) = 2.5 labor hour

With the old machine, 3 hours were the socially necessary labor time to make 1 loaf of bread, but with the new machine, the time is 2.5 labor hours, that is, half an hour less. Technological advancement has reduced the socially necessary labor time to make 1 loaf of bread. In this changed condition, if 1 loaf of bread is provided to a worker as his or her daily pay, what makes it different from the production with the old machine?

Student C: Even if they give 1 loaf of bread as daily pay like they did before, the necessary labor decreases to 2.5 labor hours. This cut necessary labor by 0.5 hour from the production with the old machine. Since the workers continue to receive 1 loaf of bread, the quality of their life doesn't go down. So, workers won't feel their wages have been reduced.

Lecturer: Right, that's what I was just going to say! Here I've explained it with bread alone, but once productive forces grow with technological advancement, not only bread but also various daily necessities such as soap, towel, toothpaste, and toothbrush have their exchange value reduced. That's because the socially necessary labor time to make those commodities is cut. With the exchange value of 1 loaf of bread decreasing to 2.5 labor hours, the necessary labor time decreases and surplus labor time increases, given daily labor of 8 hours.

8 labor hours = necessary labor (2.5 labor hours) + surplus labor (5.5 labor hours)

Even though necessary labor has been cut by 0.5 hours from 3 labor hours to 2.5 labor hours, Jim continues to receive 1 loaf of bread as his daily pay, just as he did before. This happens because the exchange value of bread has dropped due to development of productive forces. And with surplus labor increasing from 5 labor hours to 5.5 labor hours, the capitalist's profit increases. This is exactly how *relative surplus value* is produced.

Development of productive forces and relative surplus value

Student A: If improved productive forces decrease the exchange value of daily necessities such as TVs, washing machines, computers, and cell phones, it makes the perfect condition for producing *relative surplus value*.

Lecturer: That's right. Several decades ago, TVs and washing machines were luxuries only seen among rich people. Now that improved productive forces have dramatically cut the labor time necessary to produce TVs or washing machines, they're affordable to most families.

Student B: But, if the exchange value of the daily pay of 1 loaf of bread changes from 3 labor hours to 2.5 labor hours, doesn't it mean that the wage decreases from $30 to $25? This is when 1 labor hour is put at $10. In real life, however, isn't it hard to find the wage reduced just like that? If you check the wage trend, it actually suggests a steady rise.

Lecturer: There's a reason why it's difficult to recognize the reduction of necessary labor time. Technological advancement doesn't show up overnight. So, necessary labor time goes down slowly over an extended period of time. During the same period, the currency value keeps changing. When I was young, a hot dog cost 5 cents. Now, it's about $2. Over time, prices steadily rose while the currency depreciated — its value fell, making the nominal price of hot dog jump 40 fold.

Wages appear to rise steadily, but taking into account price hikes, that may not be the case. With necessary labor time decreasing, the worker's portion diminishes and the capitalist's portion increases, thus further widening the gap between rich and poor.

A great deal of statistical data shows that the gap has widened more than before. Decreases in the necessary labor time must have influenced the widening of the gap between rich and poor.

Student B: Ah..., things aren't so clear because the influence comes from multiple interconnected factors.

Lecturer: Yes, life isn't so simple. And one more thing: new technology tends to be monopolized by one company before it gets widespread and popular.

For example, Crushing Bakery develops a new bread machine and produces bread with it. With the new machine, it takes 2.5 hours (considering the raw materials and the machine) to make 1 loaf of bread. Meanwhile, at other companies it still takes 3 hours (considering the raw materials and the machine) to make 1 loaf of bread. In these circumstances, does 1 loaf of bread made by Crushing Bakery have an exchange value of 2.5 labor hours? No, it does not. It's still 3 labor hours. Why?

Crushing Bakery alone owns the new technology. So the socially necessary labor time to produce 1 loaf of bread remains 3 labor hours. This makes Crushing Bakery a *special* case. So, the exchange value of 1 loaf of bread made by Crushing Bakery remains 3 labor hours. For this reason, you should distinguish the two terms *time* and *labor time*.

Crushing Bakery, which takes 2.5 hours to make 1 loaf of bread, sells each one for $30 like other bakers do. This way, Crushing Bakery makes a *special* profit of $5. In fact, 1 loaf of bread took 2.5 hours. Thus, the excess profit that can be obtained with exclusive technology is called *extra surplus value*.

Thanks to the new technology, Crushing Bakery has enough leeway to lower the price of its product below the current market level. There's a $5 difference. The boss has a choice now. He can get a profit of $5 by keeping the same price, or he can make it more competitive by lowering the price. Even if he lowers the price by $1, there's still excess profit, so he can go further down.

Let's say that Crushing Bakery reduces its price. This puts their competing bakeries on alert. Now, they're at a crossroads: either brace for losses by lowering the price by $1 or concede defeat by surrendering their market shares to Crushing Bakery. To address the issue once and for all, they'd have to get the technology owned by Crushing Bakery. Through the withering competition, some of companies will be selected out while those who survive will end up with the same technology as Crushing Bakery has.

In the end, new technology will prevail, with one loaf of bread requiring 2.5 socially needed labor hours. This way, new technology introduced through competition shortens the labor time socially needed to make products and enables the production of relative surplus value.

Capitalist use of machines

Student B: So, competition among capitalists universalizes new technology and lowers the exchange value for commodities to produce relative surplus value. Then, is it a good thing that product values fall due to the development of new productive forces? Because workers can buy products at lower prices.

Lecturer: That's correct. Development of productive forces means that more goods can be made with less work. If a worker's wage increases in proportion to the growth of productive forces, the gap between rich and poor won't get wider.

As I said earlier, however, much statistical data points to a widening gap between rich and poor. Even if productive forces are improved, more of the benefits go to the capitalist's profit than to the worker's wage. To explain that using expressions we have learned today, the improvement of productive forces by technological development leads to the production of relative surplus value. Isn't it quite surprising that Karl Marx, who lived in the 19th century, could offer such an analysis?

Anyway, we quickly understood from the illustration using a bread bakery that even though the absolute quality of life improves for workers, the relative gap between rich and poor may get even wider. With new technology adopted, the exchange value of 1 loaf of bread decreased from 3 labor hours to 2.5 labor hours. With technology developed further, now the exchange value of 1 loaf of bread is 1 labor hour. And daily pay is 2 loaves of bread. Compared to when a worker received 1 loaf of bread, the quality of life is twice as good. But the necessary labor time has decreased to 2 labor hours, because the exchange value of 2 loaves of bread is 2 labor hours. On the other hand, surplus labor time has increased to 6 labor hours. The dropping value of daily necessities makes it possible that the *relative* gap between rich and poor widens despite the *absolute* improvement of the quality of life for workers.

Student B: *Wunderbar*. Productivity increased by technological development has intensified exploitation…. It's really intriguing that the widening gap between rich and poor is explained this way.

Actually, I had doubts if technological development would make humans any happier. What's the use of development of ICT? Companies install CCTV to monitor each and every move of workers. The conveyor belt has turned workers into cogs in a machine. I'm continually shocked to see how people destroy the environment in the name of development. Because technology has developed, people find less leisure time in their life. Now, I often wish that smartphones were gone. I ask myself if technological development is a good thing at all.

Student A: But hasn't technological development increased productive powers and so created a more affluent life for people? Of course, there are children starving throughout the world, but I think technology can serve as poison or medicine, depending how it's used.

Lecturer: Marx offered his view on technology by citing the Luddite movement in England. When England first had machines, a lot of skilled workers lost their jobs. Those angry skilled workers staged a campaign of destroying machines, and it was the famous Luddite movement.

Marx said that while he understood the anger of those skilled workers, it was misdirected. Marx thought that problems were created because the machines were used in a *capitalist* way. Machines themselves can be excellent means of liberating humankind from painful labor. When machines turn into tools strictly for creating the capitalist's profit, workers end up being cogs in the machines and are bound to perform simple repetitive tasks. Workers have to work through the night to the rhythm of the machines that operate all night. Marx believed that instead of destroying the machines, the skilled worker should fight against those *capitalists* who used the machines in an unbridled capitalist manner.

Student B: Come to think of it, I guess there was antipathy to technology itself. Because technology can bring huge benefits to humankind if it is put to better use. However, I'm afraid that workers can't avoid becoming cogs in a machine in a capitalist society where *pursuit of profit* remains the ultimate goal. And perhaps the *capitalist* use of machines as mentioned by Marx referred to the phenomenon.

Lecturer: Now you seem to understand that what essentially drives a capitalist society is pursuit of profit, which causes considerable side effects. You're following me pretty well.

Points to Ponder

- What does it mean to produce relative surplus value?

- Explain the relationship between development of productive powers and relative surplus value.

- What is extra surplus value?

- Why does the gap between rich and power widen continuously?

Lecturer: In our last lecture, we discussed the production of relative surplus value. We said that both absolute and relative surplus value were the capitalist's methods for extracting as much profit as possible from workers. By the way, there are some other methods, too. One remarkable method is to get workers to *voluntarily* subject themselves to exploitation. Simply put, it's something that drops in your lap: performance-related pay is our topic today.

Student A: I think performance-related pay is a pretty fair and desirable system, so I'm perplexed to hear that it's a cunning way to exploit people. Isn't it reasonable to get paid for your performance?

Performance-related pay is like something falling into your lap

Lecturer: A lot of people share your perception. In fact, however, it's not that simple. Many people are shocked when they hear performance-related pay described this way. Let's take a specific example to shed light on the *excellent* exploitation involved in performance-related pay.

Jim works for Piece of Cake Bakery eight hours a day to make eight loaves of bread and receives $30 as his daily pay. Then,

Piece of Cake Bakery changes its wage system, as of today. So far, everyone has been paid $30 a day regardless of how many loaves of bread they make each day. Workers have made a daily average of 8 loaves of bread, but actual output has varied with workers. Still, the company policy has maintained equal payments.

Starting today, the company implements performance-related pay and pays a specified amount of money for each loaf of bread made. If you divide the daily pay of $30 by the daily average output of 8 loaves of bread, you get $3.75 for each loaf of bread. Therefore, the company lets the workers know that they will be paid $3.75 for each loaf of bread they make. If they make 8 loaves of bread, they're paid $30 a day, but if they make 7, they're paid $26.25 and if they make 9, they're paid $33.75.

After it adopts performance-related pay, what's going to happen to Piece of Cake Bakery? As workers get extra income for each extra loaf of bread, they work harder: their labor intensity naturally increases without special enforcement and supervision.

Suppose an employee is anxious to save money for his daughter's college tuition. Previously, he made 8 loaves of bread a day. With performance-related pay in place, he makes as many as 11 loaves of bread a day by running the bread machine faster and not avoiding overtime work. As the company has made it clear that poor quality bread will be deducted from the workers' daily pay, he also pays more attention to quality.

With performance-related pay demonstrating a visible outcome, Piece of Cake Bakery announces that each month it will pick the three most productive workers and award them with a special bonus. This has created a buzz along the production line. Now craving that special bonus, every worker is hell-bent on work.

With competition intensifying, the company atmosphere undergoes some odd changes. One day, Jim's bread machine goes out of order. To get the machine fixed quickly, they need somebody's help. Jim asks his friend. However, he declines to help out, saying that now he has no time to finish his own output. He used to be perfectly willing to help, but he's a totally changed man after they adopted performance-related pay.

It's not just him; the whole company is suffused with this

atmosphere. Pursuing personal interests, those who used to be active unionists are now quite lukewarm. Everyone jumps at overtime and even weekend work. With more overtime and weekend jobs, they can get more money through performance-related pay.

Seeing the surprising changes, the boss is smiling from ear to ear. With performance-related pay, the company's productivity has remarkably increased. A worker made 8 loaves of bread a day before, and makes 10 loaves of bread now in an 8-hour workday. Previously, workers put in just 8 hours and then went home for the day, but now, they put in 10 hours on average. The magic of performance-related pay has created this change. A capitalist couldn't get a better magic spell.

Student A: Now you mention it, a business manager couldn't find a more promising method than performance-related pay. Without extra supervision, labor intensity spontaneously increases and workers simply jump at overtime and weekend shifts. I think it's pretty obvious, but I'm curious how adopting performance-related pay contributes to profits. Can we get that in numbers?

Lecturer: Certainly, it's possible. Let's take a specific example to calculate changes to profits. Remember the rate of profit formula we played with before? Let me write the formula down on here.

Rate of profit = $S/(C+V)$

C stands for constant capital (means of production) and V is for variable capital (labor power), while S represents surplus value. Now you remember. Then, shall we calculate the ratios of profit before and after performance-related pay is adopted? (In our previous calculation of the rate of profit, we treated bread machines as consumables like flour. We use the same arrangement here.)

Piece of Cake Bakery has 100 bread-making workers. Before the company adopted performance-related pay, the workers worked a daily average of 8 hours and each worker produced a daily average of 8 loaves of bread. This means, the entire workforce of 100 persons produced a total 800 loaves of bread. We calculate the exchange value of 800 loaves of bread and divide it by three components of constant capital, variable capital, and surplus value.

[Formula 1] 1kg of flour = 1 labor hour
  (amount of flour needed for 1 loaf of bread: 1kg)
[Formula 2] 1 bread machine = 10,000 labor hours
  (life of a bread machine: production of 10,000 loaves of bread)
[Formula 3] Worker's daily pay (8 hours of work) = 1 loaf of bread
  (productivity: 1 worker produces 1 loaf of bread for 1 hour)
[Formula 4] Exchange value of 8 loaves of bread
  = C(16 labor hours)+V(3 labor hours)+S(5 labor hours) = 24 labor hours

[Formula 4] By multiplying the left-handed and right-handed sides of the equation by 100, you can get a formula for 800 loaves of bread like this.

Exchange value of 800 loaves of bread = C(1,600)+V(300)+ S (500) = 2,400 labor hours

The rate of profit can be arrived at like this.

Rate of profit (without performance-related pay = S/(C+V) = 500/(1,600+300) = 5/19≈26.3%

Once performance-related pay is introduced, Piece of Cake Bakery has gotten its workers fired up in competition and their work is now stiffer. In 8 hours' work, a worker makes 10 loaves of bread on average. Other bakeries continue to let their workers make 8 loaves of bread in an 8-hour day instead of adopting performance-related pay. Under such conditions, Piece of Cake Bakery workers' 8 hours of work becomes 10 labor hours.

[Formula 5] Piece of Cake Bakery worker's 8 hours of work = 10 labor hours

Student B: Why does a Piece of Cake Bakery worker's 8 hours of work translate into 10 labor hours? Isn't it supposed to be 8 labor hours?

Lecturer: Remember, now we're talking about socially necessary labor. After Piece of Cake Bakery chose pay-per-performance, their work got harder and they do in 8 hours what workers of other companies finish in 10 hours. Working with *average* labor intensity, it still takes 10 hours to make 10 loaves of bread, but they do it in 8 hours. Hence Formulation 5. Anyway, divide the both sides of Formula 5, and you get this.

[Formula 6] Piece of Cake Bakery worker's 1 hour of work = 1.25 labor hours

Even if performance-related pay is adopted, the rate of profit remains the same

Student A: If a worker works twice as fast as before, does his 1 hour of work have the value of 2 labor hours?

Lecturer: That's right.

Let's get the rate of profit after they adopted performance-related pay.

Performance-related pay	Daily average working time	Output per hour	Daily output for the company
Before its adoption	8 hours of work	1 loaf	800 loaves
After its adoption	10 hours of work	1.25 loaves	1,250 loaves

The table shows a clear summary of the changes after performance-related pay is adopted. Before it was introduced, a worker made 1 loaf of bread each hour, and with performance-related pay, which increased labor intensity, a worker now makes 1.25 loaves of bread an hour. Moreover, before performance-related pay, workers worked average 8 hours a day, but with performance-related pay, they now work average 10 hours a day to make more money. With increased labor intensity and longer working time, the amount of bread that 100 workers produce per day increased sharply from 800 to 1,250 loaves.

It's easy to get the figure of 1,250, right? If a worker puts in 10 hours at the rate under performance-related pay, which is 1.25 loaves an hour, a worker will make 12.5 loaves of bread a day. As there are 100 workers, multiply 12.5 loaves by 100, and you get 1,250 loaves.

[Formula 4] shows the exchange value of 8 loaves of bread.

[Formula 4] Exchange value of 8 loaves of bread
= C(16 labor hours)+V(3 labor hours)+S(5 labor hours) = 24 labor hours

Then, let's calculate the exchange value of 1,250 loaves of bread with Formula 4. We divide the both sides of Formula 4 by 8 and multiply the quotient by 1,250.

[Formula 7] Exchange value of 1,250 loaves of bread
= C(2,500 labor hours)+V(468.75 labor hours)+S(781.25 labor hours) = 3,750 labor hours

The figure isn't clean but has two digits after the decimal point, a little rough. Still, the calculation is accurate.

Student A: Well, is it OK to simply get Formula 4 and do the calculation? Now they have performance-related pay which they never had before, shouldn't we check everything about it?

Lecturer: To clear up your doubts, let me try one simple calculation. Now you look at Formula 7, you see necessary labor V as 468.75 labor hours, don't you? Necessary labor is the portion of the time that a worker has put in which he or she has been paid for. Since the worker receives $3.75 for 1 loaf of bread as performance-related pay, let's multiply this by 1,250 loaves of bread and see if the product is exactly 468.75 labor hours.

On the assumption that 1 labor hour is worth $10 in money, we convert $3.75 received for 1 loaf of bread to time, and it's 0.375 labor hours. So,

$$0.375 \times 1,250 = 468.75$$

Makes sense, right?

Surplus value S can be gotten easily by subtracting C(2,500

labor hours) and V (468.75 labor hours) from 3,750 labor hours, the total value of 1,250 loaves of bread. And you know why constant capital C is 2,500 labor hours?

Student B: Yes, I know. Constant capital is what combines equipment and raw materials. 1,250 loaves of bread takes 1,250kg of flour and 1,250 labor hours and the depreciated worth of the equipment is also 1,250 labor hours, so the two combine to make 2,500 labor hours. Calculating makes things clear.

Lecturer: Now, put C(constant capital), V(variable capital), and S(surplus value) for 1,250 loaves of bread into the rate of profit formula, and you get this.

Rate of profit (with performance-related-pay) = $S/(C+V)$ = $781.25/(2,500+468.75)$ = $5/19 \approx 26.3\%$

Student A: Uh oh, the rate of profit remains the same at 26.3%, either with or without performance-related pay. So, even if performance-related pay is adopted, doesn't the capitalist get any extra profit?

Lecturer: The rate of profit figures may make you think so, but that's not really the case. Actually, the rate of profit has to remain the same. Those of you who are on the ball must have noticed it as we did the calculation. The rate of profit was calculated with Formula 4, for both 800 loaves produced a day without performance-related pay and 1,250 loaves with performance-related pay.

[Formula 4] Exchange value of 8 loaves of bread
 = C(16 labor hours)+V(3 labor hours)+S(5 labor hours) = 24 labor hours

And here's the formula to get the rate of profit. What does that tell you?

Rate of profit = $S/(C+V)$

Student A: Oh, I get it. Regardless of performance-related pay, the ratio among C, V, and S is fixed at 16:3:5, so the *rate* of profit wouldn't change. After all, we got Formula 7 by multiplying both sides of Formula 4 by the same number. But the *actual profit*. . .

Creating more profit in the same amount of time

Lecturer: Yes! The difference is clear with performance-related pay. In this example, the *Rate of profit* may not change but the *Amount of profit* changes. 100 workers produced 800 loaves of bread a day before, but now they make 1,250 loaves of bread a day. If output increases, the amount of profit increases even if the rate of profit remains the same.

If you look at Formula 7, when we analyze the value of 1,250 loaves of bread, surplus value S is 781.25 labor hours. Surplus value is the profit taken by the capitalist. When converted to money, it's $7,812.50. And as for 800 loaves of bread as the daily output before performance-related pay, we multiply both the left-handed and right-handed sides of Formula 4 by 100 like this.

Exchange value of 800 loaves of bread
= C(1,600 labor hours)+V(300 labor hours)+S(500 labor hours)
= 2,400 labor hours

Here, surplus value S is 500 labor hours, which becomes $5,000 in money. Obviously, after performance-related pay is implemented, the amount earned a day has sharply increased from $5,000 to about $7,812.50. At the same rate of profit, they make a lot more bread by increasing labor intensity and extending working time, thus creating more profit with the same workforce in the same period of time. This is possible only with performance-related pay. It's a huge difference between $5,000 and $7,812.50 earned a day, isn't it?

Student B: So that's how it works. And in an extreme case, even with the same ratio profit at 10%, the profit for a company selling $100,000,000 is 100 times bigger than that for a company selling $1,000,000. Now I see why the capitalist wants to run the factory nonstop. You have to get the factory running 24/7 not to have any down time and to get more profit.

Lecturer: Correct. By the way, I have one more thing to say.

Introducing performance-related pay, Piece of Cake Bakery said it would pay $3.75 for every loaf of bread made by a worker. What is the reason the company pays $3.75?

Student C: Before performance-related pay was introduced, the company paid the workers $30 a day. The workers make 8 loaves of bread with 8 hours of work. And by dividing $30 by 8 loaves of bread, each loaf is worth $3.75.

The rate of exploitation, and the ratio of necessary labor time and surplus labor time

Lecturer: You have a good memory. However, by playing a little trick in adopting performance-related pay, Piece of Cake Bakery may pay $3.50 instead of $3.75 for each loaf of bread. That way, the capitalist could keep more to himself or herself by cutting pay.

Since *management information* such as daily bread production isn't shared with the workers, such *tricks* are possible in shifting to performance-related pay. The workers may feel they're better off thanks to performance-related pay, they're paid more just because their labor intensity is increased and they voluntarily work overtime. So, if the company plays such tricks, the workers could actually be losing ground.

Student A: Well, it's really shocking that performance-related pay is in fact a means for strengthening voluntarily accepted exploitation. I never thought of that!

Lecturer: Generally, labor unions react pretty sharply when companies try to adopt performance-related pay. Now you've heard this, you see how it's inevitable, right? At this point, we need to discuss the *rate of exploitation*, a concept that corresponds to the rate of profit.

As I said earlier, the rate of profit is a figure that reflects *the capitalist's interests* — because it shows how much profit is generated from invested capital. On the other hand, what matters to a worker is what percentage of one's workday the time counts as necessary labor vs. surplus labor. If a lot of a day's working time goes for necessary labor, that means that a worker works largely for his own benefit. Conversely, a lot of surplus labor time suggests that the capitalist is taking a lot of time from the workers.

To illustrate this structure, Marx came up with *rate of exploitation*. Also known as *rate of surplus value*, its formula looks like this.

Rate of exploitation = S/V

The divisor V is necessary labor, and the dividend S is surplus value, see? Let's take a specific example.

8 labor hours = V(3 labor hours)+S(5 labor hours)

Rate of exploitation is calculated like this.

Rate of exploitation = S/V = $5/3 \simeq 1.67 \simeq 167\%$

If necessary labor and surplus value are 4 labor hours each, what is the rate of exploitation?

8 labor hours = V(4 labor hours)+S(4 labor hours)

Rate of exploitation = S/V = $4/4 = 1 = 100\%$

Here we can see that as necessary labor increases and surplus value go down, the rate of exploitation decreases from 1.67 to 1. The rate of exploitation is a recurrent concept, so keep it in mind.

With the concept of the rate of exploitation, we can see that the worker's portion of the wage and the capitalist's portion of the wage are in opposition. To increase wages when working time is fixed would require increasing the necessary working time. That would make the surplus value (the capitalist's portion) go down. On the contrary, decreasing the necessary working time increases surplus value. After all, the worker's profit and the capitalist's profit are fundamentally at each other's expense. One party's profit means the other party's loss. This is exactly why frequent conflicts are bound to occur between employees and capitalists.

Student A: I'm starting to wonder whether I should get a job.

If workers understand the content of *Das Kapital*, they should feel pretty much trapped. I guess they would hate working for a company. Nonetheless, I have to get a job because I have no choice ....

Student B: I think it's true that exploitation exists in a capitalist society. But capitalists aren't just loafing around, themselves, are they? Capitalists too work hard and do business by taking risks in investing. Isn't that recognized? Frankly, can companies operate without capitalists?

Lecturer: Didn't we hear similar talk in the previous lecture? Of course, many capitalists work hard. I'm not saying that capitalists should not receive the value of their work. However, our society clearly has a huge gap between rich and poor that cannot be explained by the competence gap. And Marx theorizes on the fundamental cause for this situation.

And what is common sense today may be nonsense tomorrow. Should capitalists alone own factories? Workers can jointly own a factory. In fact, in some countries there are cooperative unions that provide for workers' shared ownership. Workers in a cooperative, who are its co-owners, work together on equal footing, and they hold a general assembly to make important decisions by vote, and distribute profits evenly. Workers also elect their CEO. Which is the more democratic structure — the capitalist corporation where one single person decides everything or the cooperative as a joint operation by workers?

Student A: Of course, the cooperative would be more democratic. Now, I can imagine students voting for their class president, but I've never heard of workers electing their CEO. Maybe, the capitalist business system is an outdated, undemocratic system entirely...

Lecturer: Of course, such cooperatives also operate within the system of capitalism, so they have to pursue profits to survive market competition. And many cases reveal the limitations of the model. Still, they're run in a little bit more democratic way. By comparison, the capitalist system is a far cry from democracy.

Today, we've dealt with performance-related pay. For now, I think we're done with formulas and in our next session, we'll have some more general discussions.

Points to Ponder:

- How does performance-related pay influence work conditions?

- When the rate of profit remains the same, why would they introduce performance-related pay?

- What is the "rate of exploitation"?

- Why do the workers' interests clash with those of the capitalist?

LECTURE 8 — SELFISH PEOPLE ARE ADAPTED TO A CAPITALIST SOCIETY

Lecturer: With all that we've uncovered in our seven lectures so far, you must have sustained a considerable shock. This kind of knowledge is not found in everyday discourse. Some of you must be confused, while others may find the content objectionable. That's understandable. When I first read the book in college, I felt the kind of shock that Neo in *Matrix* had when he saw how the world really looked by taking the red pill.

However, even after they understand *Das Kapital*, many people seem to think this way: "I know there are a lot of problems with capitalism. But, no system is perfect in this world. Human beings are by nature selfish. A society in which selfish people live will inevitably be driven by selfishness...."

Student A: In fact, that's exactly what I think.

Lecturer: Yes, people think in a pretty similar way. Someone usually brings up some cliché about human nature being good or evil.

Today, we begin with human nature. A lot of people consider humans selfish by nature and they feel resigned to that.

Is human nature evil?

Student B: Once a classmate of mine was out sick one day, and he asked to borrow my notes. I made some excuse not to give them to him. He was doing better than me in school. I justified myself by thinking, "Everybody looks after his own interests first, after all." But I felt a little bad about it....

Student C: Of course, it's natural to take care of yourself, isn't it?

Lecturer: If selfishness were part of human nature, humans should have selfishness carved into their DNA, right? Let's see if that's the case.

Let's talk about a newborn baby who just came out of the mother's womb and has its first encounter with this world. Actually, raising two children, I've realized many things about human beings.

One day while my wife was pregnant with our first child, she was reading a book on child rearing and she asked me a question.

"When a newborn baby poops, the parent takes care of it. But this book says that even as it watches the parent do the cleaning, the baby thinks that he (or she) is doing the cleaning. Why is that?"

The book didn't explain such thinking on the part of the newborn. Can anyone guess?

Student A: I've heard that babies aren't able to distinguish themselves from others. Is this related?

Lecturer: That sounds quite plausible. Let's think it through. Let's say that a baby who just came out of the womb is looking at the people who are around. Can the baby really interpret humans as *humans*?

Student A: Of course, the baby will see humans as humans. What kind of question is that?

Student B: If a baby is encountering the world for the first time, how would the baby know to think of humans as humans?

Lecturer: You're a sharp thinker. When we see a combination of certain colors and shapes, we usually recognize it as a human being, but that's not a congenital faculty. For a newborn baby, everything that comes into sight is just a meaningless combination of colors and shapes. The baby has no way of knowing that a combination of certain colors and shapes represents a dog, a cat, a person, or an apartment. Just as you can't find a meaning in a snow screen, a newborn baby cannot interpret the combination of certain colors and shapes as a human. It's all meaningless!

Have you ever seen a newborn baby bundled in swaddling clothes so that it can't move its arms?

Student A: Yes, I saw my recently born nephew all bundled up. With just his face peeking out, he looked so cute, but it was so sad, too.

Lecturer: Do you know why they wrap babies so completely to keep their arms from moving?

Student A: I've heard that otherwise, they might scratch their faces, but I don't understand. Why would they scratch their own faces?

Lecturer: Newborn babies fail to recognize that the things with five fingers now seen in their eyes are their arms. They're seeing them for the first time. They don't even know that they can control the arms with their will. The arms just move reflexively. So, when the arms move close to their face, they don't know how to get them away. Within a short time after birth, babies often place their fists right before their faces and play by moving them slightly. It's then that they vaguely realize that they can control the fists that they see. They're happy moving their fists as if controlling game characters.

Student A: Oh, cool! How do you know that?

Lecturer: Haha, I've never done any special study on newborns. I realized while thinking deeply how the world would be perceived by a newborn baby.

To understand the psychology of a newborn, you have to learn one more thing. Let's say there's a desk in front of you. Now you reach out and touch the desk, you can feel it, right? And you think that the tactile sense on your hand originates from the desk. So, you feel that the manually perceived tactile sense and the image of the desk in your eyes are one and the same thing.

However, tactile sense and visual sense are two different things. Suppose that we have no eyes. Could we connect the manually perceived tactile sense with the visual image? With no eyes available, tactile sense is mere tactile sense, and the visual images of a desk or a soft cotton comforter cannot be connected to the touches. Then, what makes us identify the touch of hardness with the visual image of the desk? It's the brain. From continuous experience, we start to perceive a close connection between the visual image captured in a specific location and the touch through your hand.

This should help you understand why the newborn thinks that it has taken care of its poop. See, the newborn has pooped. Feeling uncomfortable, the baby cries. This gets the parent to move closer, wondering why. Newborns have no such concepts as *parent* or *person*. As the parent approaches, the newborn perceives it as certain colors and shapes showing on the screen. To change diapers for the baby, the parents will move their hands busily, carefully wiping the child with wet wipes. While the baby sees the movement of the parents' hands, the child has no idea that their movement is connected with the touch on the butt. While colors loudly move around before its eyes, something touches its behind and the poop suddenly disappears.

The baby now thinks that when it cried, the colors changed, the touch appeared, and the poop disappeared. It's like the magician's incantation working the magic in a role-playing game.

Student C: But, is there any connection between the newborn's poop and Why are we talking about babies?

Lecturer: You'll see. Perceiving the world this way, newborns cannot distinguish themselves from external objects. They just relate various data perceived through sense organs to themselves. So, they think that they have put away the poop. And when a baby poops and cries, the parent doesn't always show up right away. For instance, if the parents are asleep, no matter how long the baby cries over its poop, the specific color pattern (the parent) won't show on screen. As such experiences pile up, the baby begins to realize that the specific color pattern is an *outside* presence that is beyond its voluntary control. That is how the distance (separation) between subject and object comes into being. And *self-identity* is formed in the distance between subject and object. Previously, there was no distinction between me and them, so there was no such psychological entity as *me*, but with the distance from other forming, the self develops.

Thus the self-identity of *me* develops from the relationship with other. Without the other, I cannot exist. Without you, there is no me, either. You have no memory of when you were one year old. Why is that so? If you couldn't signify colors and shapes, how can you remember those days? Since there is no signifying what I saw, what I heard, and what I smelled, I can't remember, either. But you have some dim memories of when you were about four years old. That's because our brain matures enough to enable the mental activity called *memory* at about that time.

Anyway, newborns have no concept of *selfishness*. When there is no distinction between me and you, a high-level consciousness like selfishness should be out of the question. Thus, the statement that humans are evil by nature simply betrays insufficient understanding of human psychological development.

Humans think through neural network, a collection of neurons, the nerve cells. If we compare the neural network that is found in the adult brain to the nationwide network of the roads, the neural network of a newborn is as simple as expressways. Most of the neural network is formed postnatally through interactions with surrounding environment.

Social structure forms human psychology

Student A: Ah, so you mean, the concept of selfishness doesn't even exist in a newborn baby. That makes sense.

Lecturer: Right. All living organisms basically have a survival instinct. To understand human psychology, we must begin with the survival instinct. After all, categorical imperatives for all living organisms are *survival* and *reproduction*. Why are appetite and sexual desire too strong to suppress? Appetite is related to survival, whereas sexual desire is related to reproduction. If some bio organism is genetically destitute of appetite and sexual desire, it is unlikely to survive and reproduce; it is likely to go extinct. Strong appetite and sexual desire are psychological outcomes of the evolution of bio organisms.

By the way, psychological virtues needed for survival vary depending on what environment and social structure we live in. Here, let me introduce to you an impressive case that I encountered in a book. A Western anthropologist who lived in a capitalist society performed an intelligence test on a Native American tribe. Handing test sheets out to individual tribesmen, the academic virtually begged them to act independently in solving the problems. However, the Native American tribes-men huddled with one another to solve the problems. So, the frustrated anthropologist approached them and emphasized that they should work separately in solving the problems. The Native Americans said, "When there are problems, shouldn't we discuss them to find solutions? We don't understand why you keep telling us to work separately."

How come the Native Americans think that way? *A primitive community* can hardly survive without helping one another. Obtaining food through hunting and gathering, and sharing child care, the community members have to work together. That alone could increase their survival rate. Naturally, *cooperation* instead of selfishness becomes an important virtue for survival in a primitive community. People quickly share knowledge and information they have acquired with other community members and even share the food they get through hunting and sharing. If group members fail to help one another out of selfishness, their survival rate should drop sharply.

Student A: Quite a contrast with the capitalist society. This suggests that instead of human nature being selfish, the social structure plays a big part in forming human psychology.

Lecturer: That's right. In a capitalist society, people pursue profits. The capitalist exploits workers to get more money. It is to survive market competition that the capitalist struggles for ever more money. If a company fails to make more profit than other companies, it is bound to drop out of market competition. This is the game rule for the capitalist society.

Even if workers are hurt, the capitalist can readily hire temp workers and increase profits by reducing wages. If they can save money by not installing filters and secretly letting waste water flow into the river, capitalists will do it. By the rules of the capitalist game, you have to do so to get more profits and become the winner.

If workers can't sell their labor power, they have difficulty surviving and breeding. Because the means of production are in the capitalist's hands, all workers have is their body. In a primitive community, people lived by sharing what they get through hunting and gathering — whereas, in the capitalist society, a person is left alone to deal with everything. Your sick child has to be treated on your money, and you have to pay for your child's school education.

In a capitalist society, where one has to do everything on one's own, selfishness alone can be one's savior. If you rashly consider others and put yourself in their shoes, you fall behind and can end up vulnerable. Those who shrewdly stick to their interests get the first promotion and make good money. To survive, you have to grovel to your superiors and you have to play the game, even if you get mistreated and even insulted.

And as people who have had their brush with this aspect of life, parents advise their children to become professionals like doctors or lawyers who make good money. They simply don't want to let their children repeat the same woes in a worker's life that requires them to debase themselves. Understandably, they take a stern hand with their children, stressing that they have to work hard in school and go to a good college, since you're likelier to become a professional if you have a diploma from a good college.

The rules of the capitalist game naturally percolate into *schools.* In the most competitive environments, like New York City, ambitious parents fight to get their tiny children into the "best" nursery schools in order to get them into the best private prep schools, in order to smooth the way to the best universities and grad schools. Children may find themselves being assigned tutors and sent to voluntary evening study and SAT prep classes. That's on top of athletics and "leadership" and community involvement activities. You have to beat your buddies and get higher scores if you want to go to your preferred college. Students may end up with a lot of stress.

Is it wrong? Who, as parents, would want to see their child taking it easy, only to be saddled later with the drudgery and insecurity of a worker's life? It's the rules of the capitalist game that force us all to be selfish.

Student A: I guess I'm dumb. Life is so fleeting, even when we help one another and look on the bright side only .... But, society can't simply return to the stage of a primitive community, right?

Student B: Can't we just change the rules of the game? If we live like this, our minds will be devastated, won't they? I sometimes think that capitalism is driving our society over a cliff.

Environmental degeneration, destruction of humanity, endless wars.... So many wars are ultimately launched in order for someone to make money. Even the desire to defend one's wealth brings wars....

> *Fetishism, the idea that money can buy anything, is a phenomenon peculiar to capitalism*

Lecturer: In a capitalist society, money talks. If you have a lot of money, you can wear good clothes, eat good food, and get a pretty or good-looking dating partner even if you don't work. Wherever you go, you'll be received like a king if only you've got money. People who have committed crimes can avoid punishment if they've got enough money. Poor people have to do time in jail, even if they steal things because they're hungry. *Money* can buy *anything* in a capitalist society. That's the reality of a society that commoditizes everything.

But come to think of it, the idea that money talks is a kind of *fantasy*. Money, that is, the paper with the image of a national leader printed on it, has no ability at all.

Let's suppose that from this moment forward, people don't do anything but lie around at home. No products will be produced. The paper with the image of a national leader printed on it can no longer be suddenly turned into a TV.

All the goods we buy with money are products of someone's labor. Unless farmers work, food is not produced. Unless construction workers work, this classroom where we study wouldn't be here. If engineers don't work, smartphones won't be around, either. How grateful should we be for this process? Thanks to the labor of other people, we can wear clothes, eat food, and use our smartphones.

I can live like a human being thanks to other people's labor. Of course, other people should benefit from my labor. Without other people's help, our life can't exist. Money merely serves as the medium for the exchange of labor. After all, we're members of a labor community in which we rely on one another.

However, the capitalist society downgrades *other people's labor* — which is precious and we should be thankful for it — to simple figures in money. It replaces a warm *human* relationship with a cold *moneyed* relationship.

As a child, I frequently heard from my parents that if you didn't finish your food at the table, you were inviting trouble. As I got older, I somehow began to refute this. I once thought, what's so wrong with leaving some food, when we've paid for it? But if it were my parents who grew the food in the field, working since early morning without even stopping to stretch, I wouldn't have thrown it away so casually. You can't handle it so carelessly if you know what efforts it took for your food to arrive at your table.

In a capitalist society, a worker's labor is covered up, leaving a money-indicated price instead. This carrot is 50 cents, this shaver is $5...and so on. Thus, you can't properly feel gratitude for the value of other people's labor.

Marx referred to *fetishism* in his book. It means that matter has become a god. A god is an all-powerful being. In the Middle Ages, God's will was used to justify things, no matter how nonsensical they looked, for example, a witch hunt or a crusade. Now, money takes the position of an all-powerful God in a capitalist society where everything is commoditized. Money reigns over everything, and for money, nonsensical things are justified. And money recognizes no parents.

Student A: In those terms, fetishism does seem to be rampant. Goodness knows for how long we've been accustomed to pricing things. When a dam construction fails, they say, *$10 billion* damage is expected. What would be the price of a migratory bird, or a tree? Movies are evaluated on the "box office," not the talent. Human organs like eyeballs or kidneys are given prices and traded. They even say how much a date with an entertainment celebrity costs. You're considered eccentric unless you pursue money in a society where money gets you anything.

Lecturer: That's life in a capitalist society, so it's hard to say that we shouldn't be selfish or we shouldn't think of money only. Humans aren't selfish by nature but are trained to be selfish by the rules of the capitalist game. Because you have to live, no matter how.

We find such a life natural, as a matter of course, but not everyone does. Most countries, including paragons of capitalism like Australia and Singapore, and almost all of Europe, have achieved universal health insurance at far less cost than the U.S. People are shocked to see how much we have to pay for doctors and medications. Canadians who spend their winters in the U.S. are frightened enough to take out a special insurance policy, just in case they have an injury or illness while they're here.

This is a phenomenon peculiar to a capitalist society

Lecturer: There's an academic discipline called evolutionary psychology. It studies human psychology from the perspective of evolutionary theory. Human psychology is ultimately the product of metabolism performed by the lump of proteins called the brain. Humans have evolved over time while adapting to the environment in a way more favorable to their survival and breeding, and the brain as well must have been carved to be fitter for survival and breeding through its evolution. So, to correctly understand human psychology which results from brain activity, we should get at the human psychology involved in the human evolution that has increased probability of survival and breeding through adjusting to the environment.

Humans have a desire for recognition, which is as instinctive as the desire for food and sexual desire. Company workers are recognized by their bosses, students are recognized by parents and teachers, politicians are recognized by the public, social activists are recognized by their colleagues.... As if recognition were to spirit what food is to body, humans thirst for recognition.

But why is it that our instincts include the desire for recognition? From the perspective of evolutionary psychology, humans lack the strong muscles or paws of a tiger and the quick feet of a rabbit. So, we humans recognize our vulnerability. Humans came to live in herds, through evolution. For many individuals, being excluded from one's group is practically a death sentence. It's a terrifying situation that one has to avoid.

To avoid being excluded from a group, it is imperative to get *recognized* by others. Recognition decreases the probability of being excluded but increases the probability of survival and breeding. Then, one can leave one's DNA to posterity. Perhaps that trace of the desire for recognition has been left by the continuation of such a way of life through our evolution. A tiger doesn't need to seek recognition from others.

From the perspective of evolutionary psychology, humans aren't selfish by nature. On the contrary, humans have a community-oriented DNA that craves recognition from a group. In a capitalist system, however, people have to serve *money* more than *community* to survive and breed. Thrown into this system that commoditizes everything, one puts one's bank balance above one's sense of belonging to the community.

Too bad, we aren't tigers. We're *humans* and we have evolved in such a way that we have to live on the spiritual food called recognition from the community. People can't find a true sense of belonging to a community in money-based relationships. You can get some degree of recognition from people for the money you have, but that's applicable to rich people only. In a capitalist society, most people feel alienated as they lack spiritual food demanded at the DNA level; and at the worst, they suffer from *spiritual malnutrition* such as depression and panic disorder. In fact, that is true of rich people, too. When they realize that people just love their money, not them, they suffer from a spiritual thirst that can't be satisfied.

This is exactly why we see a lot of spiritually unstable people lately. The capitalist system that boosts selfishness and fetishism is totally out of line with the human instinctive attachment to communal life, which has formed through the long time of human evolution. And this disharmony appears as a mental disorder.

Student A: I hadn't noticed that humans are instinctively attracted to community instead of being selfish by nature. Then, as long as the capitalist social structure persists, is there no hope for humankind? Will human society get sick with everyone enslaved to selfishness and fetishism?

Lecturer: Humans aren't like robots that are forged by their given environment. Robots lack feelings, whereas humans have emotions. If such a society continues, most people will feel more sorrow and anger than happiness and joy. People will realize something's wrong and try to figure out why. The emotions of anger and sorrow, and rational analysis of an issue, change a person's behavior. Because, while we're affected by the environment, we humans can change the environment with our free hands.

The capitalist society clearly has more merits than the previous forms of society. But this isn't the end of the story. We should address the contradictions of the capitalist society and advance to a stage where people can live happily. It is up to all of us now to realize that other people's labor is as precious as our own and create a community where we respect one another and happily mix. Such a society would build on our innate desire to belong to a community.

Points to Ponder

- Are humans selfish by nature?
- Are people bound to be selfish in a capitalist society?
- What is fetishism?
- How can the human nature be explained from the perspective of evolutionary psychology?

Lecture 9 — How Does a Capitalist Use Profit?

Lecturer: Today, let's talk about how a capitalist uses profit.

M–C(LP, MP)–P–C'–M'

Now we're back with the general formula for capital. Just in case, let me repeat: at the outset, a capitalist buys means of production MP and labor power LP with money M. Production process P makes commodity C' to sell on the market, which process comes up with surplus value as the source of profit. When the produced commodity C' is sold on the market, money M' is earned. Earned money M' is bigger than start-up capital. This is because surplus value is created with a worker's surplus labor in the production process P.

Simple reproduction and expanded reproduction

Lecturer: How does the capitalist use his or her earned profit?
Student A: Maybe to buy a nice house and eat at fancy restaurants? And international travel, too. If I were rich, that's what I'd do.
Lecturer: Yes, that's what many of them do; on the other hand, though, some live a modest life.
Piece of Cake Bakery makes a profit of $5,000 a day, but the

boss is such a spendthrift that he squanders just as much every day. He pays $200 for dinner and burns thousands of dollars at posh nightclubs. He gambles and he shows off, throwing huge parties. You wouldn't believe the car he drives. Or should I say, cars.

Now, let me describe how profits are spent through an individual capitalist's consumption, as in his case, with the general formula for capital.

$$M–C(LP, MP)–P–C'–M' \ (= M+m)$$

The profit of $5,000 that the owner of Piece of Cake Bakery gets each day is m. As he squanders the profit on his luxurious life, there is no money left to invest in new machines or to expand the factory. If a factory is run like this, the business size doesn't change; it maintains the same size. Like this.

Cycle 1: $M–C(LP, MP)–P–C'–M'(= M+m)$
Cycle 2: $M–C(LP, MP)–P–C'–M'(= M+m)$
Cycle 3: $M–C(LP, MP)–P–C'–M'(= M+m)$
Cycle 4: $M–C(LP, MP)–P–C'–M'(= M+m)$

Cycle 1, Cycle 2, Cycle 3, and Cycle 4 show the repetition of the series of processes in which the capitalist makes bread and makes money by selling it in the market. As long as the company stays in business, this circuit can go on without end. The company size undergoes no change, while workers repeat their routine operation. This way, production of the same size continuously repeated without reinvestment is referred to as *simple reproduction.*

Unlike the owner of Piece of Cake Bakery, the owner of Crushing Bakery saves most of his profit of $5,000. He eats at the company cafeteria. Unmarried and with no children, he doesn't have to spend his money for anything. He avoids ostentatious entertaining. And he's got no interest in golf. Instead, he invests all the profits in new machinery and in more flour, and hiring more employees, and he makes his business bigger. In this way, his profit grows day after day. This is what the following formulas show.

Cycle 1: M–C–M'(= M+m)
Cycle 2: M'–C'–M' '(= M'+m)
Cycle 3: M' '–C' '–M' ' '(= M' ' +m)
Cycle 4: M' ' '–C' ' '–M' ' ' '(= M' ' ' +m)

Begun as M in Cycle 1, the capital grows to M' as Cycle 1 comes to an end. As it passes Cycle 2 through reinvesting the profit, the capital grows even further to M' '. As this process continues, business size gets bigger and bigger. Capital grows in size with profit reinvested is referred to as *expanded reproduction*.

Of course, in real life, it's difficult to expand a business before you pull together some significant profits. When it takes $100,000 to buy one more bread machine, it takes a long time to get the budget for purchasing the machine with the daily profit of $5,000. So, as shown in the example, capital doesn't get bigger with every cycle. You can invest in facilities only if you put aside a certain amount of profit. To describe how simple reproduction and expanded reproduction differ, the process has been simplified.

Student A: Simple reproduction reflects what happens when profits earned by the capitalist are never reinvested. The business size remains the same while turning like a squirrel in a wheel. On the other hand, expanded reproduction is what the capitalist does to make business bigger by actively reinvesting his profits. Is there such a thing as *reduced reproduction*? I guess somehow reduced reproduction should exist to complete the set.

Lecturer: Yes. Reduced reproduction refers to the situation in which a business goes bad and its capital is exhausted; company size thus diminished. This is the most undesirable situation.

Profit being continuously reinvested into capital is referred to as *capital accumulation*. Capital accumulation will go on forever so long as the capitalist society continues, because all successful capitalists will continue to reinvest their profits in pursuit of greater profits.

Student C: With all the strange terminology pouring in all of a sudden, it's pretty mind-boggling.

Organic composition of capital

Lecturer: We have more coming. You only have to follow me step by step. Nothing to worry about.

Now, let's check the concept of *organic composition of capital*. I'll first talk about how technological development influences the production line.

In an earlier lecture, I mentioned the Luddite Movement which took place in England. I described it as a massive action by skilled workers who had lost their jobs to newly invented machines; they set out to destroy those machines. Some 200 years later, workers are suffering similar damage from technological development. So, a labor union which negotiates a collective bargain with the company sometimes inserts a clause that requires the company to discuss the introduction of new technology with the union. When capital accumulation or expanded reproduction proceeds, exactly what influence is technological development going to exert?

Crushing Bakery invests $10 million in production. He invests $2 million to purchase flour and bread machine as constant capital C and $8 million to purchase variable capital V of labor power. And the ratio of constant capital C against variable capital V is calculated as 0.25.

$$\text{Organic compositon of capital (OCC)} = C/V = 20/80 = 1/4 = 0.25$$

This ratio of constant capital C against variable capital V is called the organic composition of capital (OCC). Roughly speaking, it's the ratio of facility investment against labor cost in investment cost. As $8 million out of an invested fund of $10 million is labor cost, this is very *labor-intensive*.

Thirty years later, Crushing Bakery invests an extra $10 million. In the meantime, a newly invented machine has replaced the workers. The owner and CEO of Crushing Bakery has spent $8 million out of his invested $10 million to buy flour and bread machines and $2 million to hire workers. He has spent $8 million to buy constant capital C and $2 million to buy variable capital V. Then, shall we calculate the organic composition of capital?

OCC = C/V = 80/20 = 4/1 = 4

The organic composition of capital sharply increased from 0.25 to 4. This means that the portion of facility investment in the invested fund of $10 million has greatly increased. This increasing ratio of constant capital C against variable capital V is called *the rising organic composition of capital*. It means that as more efficient equipment is developed, labor costs diminish in the invested fund while facility investment increases.

Student A: Industrial structure changes from *labor-intensive industry* to *technology-intensive industry*. Then, employment, or rather unemployment, will get serious, won't it? The ratio of labor cost in investment cost decreases sharply.

Lecturer: If the organic composition of capital rises, workers clearly tend to be driven out of jobs. Marx called people who can't find jobs and remain unemployed *reserve army of labor*.

While it is perplexing to people who can't find jobs, the presence of reserve army of labor is helpful to the capitalist. With a large reserve army of labor available, a capitalist can easily get replacement workforce, so he has the upper hand over workers in negotiation. Thus, even during rapid inflation, a capitalist can easily get needed workers at wages he finds convenient. When a society is close to full employment, a capitalist can't find replacement workers so easily. The capitalist will be at a disadvantage in negotiating with workers. Of course, when workers know that the capitalist can't easily fire them, they can bravely assert their rights. If it's hard to get workers, the capitalist can't increase production much, no matter how vibrant the economy is.

Student A: These days, youth unemployment is a big problem, and the talk of reserve army of labor is even more depressing. If you're right, the presence of unemployed people in a capitalist society may be inevitable.

Lecturer: Quite depressing, but that's the reality. No obligation can force a capitalist to hire workers. Capitalists hire workers so long as that helps create his profit. Those who don't help create the capitalist's profit will be found unworthy of their food.

Anyway, in the course of capital accumulation, as new technologies are introduced with technological development, the size of the reserve army of labor and the number of poor people go up. Marx called the phenomenon *the absolute general law of capitalist accumulation.*

Who should own the means of production?

Students: .... (depressed)

Lecturer: With a reserve army of labor, the whole classroom looks pretty down. Don't worry. You'll all get a job.

Today, we discussed how the capitalist uses his or her profit and learned more about simple reproduction, expanded reproduction, organic composition of capital, and reserve army of labor. I have one more thing to say before I finish the lecture. It's important, so please pay attention.

The boss of Crushing Bakery now wonders where to invest his profit of $10 million. Money making isn't easy in the bread industry, which is saturated now, so he is considering going into a new area. And when he heard there was a sudden surge of Chinese tourists, he considered going into the tourism business; and now he's speculating as to how artificial intelligence might give him an edge. A buddy tipped him off about some land that's been slated to be developed sooner or later, so he's attracted to real estate investing now. When the workers at Crushing Bakery asked him to spend a portion of his profit on the company's benefits for workers, he firmly refused, insisting that the company management is solely his and it's none of their business. As a capitalist, he decides everything for the company just like a dictator.

Samsung Group once went into the auto industry and pulled out after it suffered huge losses. It was a case in which a major investor insisted on an investment that moved several tens of billion dollars and had a major influence on the whole national economy. At the time, the Korean auto industry was already saturated. By investing in the auto industry just because of the *chaebol* magnate's desire, Samsung Group inflicted an enormous damage on the Korean economy. If the money was spent instead on benefits like free healthcare, it would have been a great contribution to the society. However, capitalists generally don't invest their profits in something like that. That's because it doesn't help them make money. Important decisions are always left to capitalists. Have you ever heard that workers were asked where to invest a company's profits?

From a social perspective, banks play a larger role than ordinary companies do in investment. Banks attract the spare funds of families and companies as deposits, and they lend to families or companies at interest. Part of the interest return to the depositors, while the remaining sum is kept by banks. Thus, banks enjoy enormous power in deciding to whom to lend their huge money. Countless companies are dying to get loans from banks. Weak companies may not survive without bank loans. And banks place top priority on profit in considering their loans. Have you ever heard that banks provided loans for free healthcare and free education?

Student A: If capitalists decide everything, then in effect they're the owners of the society. I think that the more pressing and important things for people are healthcare, education, and housing. A family with a cancer patient will be completely destroyed. Because of tuition costs, college students and their parents are struggling. Housing prices are exorbitant. If social resources and finances were used to solve such problems, it would help a lot of people.

But capitalists are interested in making money, and they don't seem to pay attention to the basic welfare of the people. Of course, it's a good thing to earn money. But it is a problem that money earned like that is used solely to serve only the capitalists' interests. The wealth enjoyed by corporate owners originates from the surplus value created by workers. Companies can operate without financial speculators, but for now, they need workers. Nonetheless, a capitalist society operates solely in the interests of the biggest capitalists.

Student B: But, aren't companies supposed to pursue profits? I mean, those companies that don't try to make more profit are going to be selected out and face bankruptcy. When there's no profit being created, you can't produce goods any longer.

Lecturer: That's correct. In a capitalist system, companies have to pursue profits. Where there's no profit, you can't go on making products. Before the capitalist society, profit didn't matter — people did farming and made things for their living. Just think if you had some reason for making stuff. Let's say, ten people are building wooden cabins to have a cozy life. Do they think about profits? Isn't it just for their own comfortable life that they're building them? People can produce things even when they make no profits. Since we're used to the capitalist system, we just believe that profit is the sole objective of production. It is human labor and not profit that creates value.

In a capitalist society, capitalists can decide like dictators because they monopolize means of production such as land, machines, and raw materials. It's quite like feudal lords owning manors and wielding power. The state system in a capitalist society protect the capitalist's power in the name of protection of private properties. People who don't have means of production can only sell their labor power to capitalists to make a living. And in such a socioeconomic structure, it isn't easy to have a democracy. So, power will concentrate in the few capitalists.

Marx thought that we would need to do something about the ownership of the means of production if we wanted to realize democracy. He believed that people had to create a world in which workers escape their exploitation as wage slaves, get respected as agents of productive activities, and have a hand in the decision-making process. He thought that to make this happen, people had to change the capitalist's monopoly over the means of production to community ownership.

In Marx's view, common ownership of the means of production can promote the community's well-being without wasting a society's resources and funds on private interests and desires. Then, there would be no laying off workers or stopping production due to unprofitable operation alone. If people could work in proportion to their needs, they wouldn't have to work unnecessarily long hours. Industrial disasters would be greatly reduced and environmental pollution would diminish, too. If the goal of production were not to create profits, there would be no profit calculation, either.

In such a society, Jim's eight hours of daily work as a bread-making worker would change as follows.

[In the capitalist society] daily 8 hours' work = necessary labor (3 labor hours)+surplus labor (5 labor hours)

[In the new society] daily 8 hours' work = necessary labor (8 labor hours)

In such a society, everything that people produce is returned as the community's benefits, so all 8 hours of daily work are applied to necessary labor.

Student A: While Marx's argument sounds like a fantasy, it would be nice if we could get closer to such a society. Because I think the current merciless capitalism can't work in the long run.

Lecturer: The biggest problem with a capitalist society is that the system makes it hard to realize democracy. Of course, Marx's idea may sound fanciful. But remember, historical progress is achieved when a dream turns into a reality. In the United States, it wasn't until the 1920s that women got the right to vote. Before the 1920s, women's suffrage was a fantasy. Of course, it takes countless people's efforts and struggles to turn a dream into a reality.

Points to Ponder

- Describe the meaning of simple reproduction and expanded reproduction and explain the difference.

- What does it mean that the organic composition of capital rises?

- What's the reason that reserve army of labor is needed by capitalists?

- Why is it that capitalism and democracy are incompatible?

LECTURE 10 — CAPITALISTS FIGHT OVER SURPLUS VALUE

Lecturer: Today, we're going to learn what capital *turnover* means, and how different *fractions* of capital fight over the surplus value taken away from workers.

$$M–C(LP, MP)–P–C'–M'$$

Remember the general formula for capital? Now you've seen it several times, I think you're pretty familiar with it. Still, let me explain the different processes of the formula to make sure you understand it completely.

$M–C(LP, MP)$: circulation process
The process in which a capitalist purchases labor power (LP) and means of production (MP) with money

P: production process
The process in which new commodities are produced with means of production and labor power

$C'–M'$: circulation process
The process in which commodities made through production process are converted to money by selling them to the market

As start-up capital M goes through M–C(LP, MP)–P–C'–M', profit accrues and money M' increases. Now, let's consider the concept of *time* in a series of processes. The owner of Piece of Cake Bakery starts his business with his start-up capital M of $1,000,000. And the times it takes to run once through the process of M–C(LP, MP)–P–C'–M' is as follows.

M–C(LP, MP): 1 month
The time it takes to purchase labor power (LP) and the means of production (MP) with capital (M)

P: 5 months
The time it takes to produce commodities

C'–M': 6 months
The time it takes to convert commodities to money by selling them to the market

In this model, it takes 1 month plus 5 months plus 6 months, that is 1 year to complete the course of M–C(LP, MP)–P–C'–M'. Provided the rate of profit for Piece of Cake Bakery is 20%, 1 billion won M will grow to $1,200,000 M' in a year.

Turnover time of capital and annual rate of profit

In a capitalist society, the purpose of a company is to create more profits at the minimum cost in the shortest period of time. What changes will happen if the time required for the process is shortened?

M–(LP, MP): 1 month
P: 2 months
C'–M': 3 months

The time required for the process of M–C(LP, MP)–P–C'–M' is shortened to 6 months (1 month plus 2 months plus 3 months). 1 year has been cut short to 6 months. When the process of M–C(LP, MP)–P–C'–M' is completed, the rate of profit remains the same 20% as before. Start-up capital M of $1,000,000 becomes $1,200,000 M' in six months. The profit, $200,000 out of $1,200,000 is deposited at the bank for future investment, and the remaining $1,000,000 goes through the process of M–C(LP, MP)–P–C'–M' and earns an extra profit of $200,000 in six months. Previously, 1 year made $200,000, but with time shortened for different processes, $400,000 is earned in the same period of time.

This way, capital regularly repeats the specific circuit M–C(LP, MP)–P–C'–M', a regularly repeated circuit that is called capital turnover. The time it takes to complete one circuit is the *turnover time* of capital. In the example I just showed, the turnover time of capital was reduced from 1 year to 6 months. As a result, the profit doubled in the same period.

Student C: So, even if the rate of profit is fixed at 20%, the profit varies depending how many times the process of M–C(LP, MP)–P–C'–M' is completed in the same period. The faster the turnover, the greater the profit becomes in proportion to the number of times.

Lecturer: Exactly for that reason, Marx came up with the concept of the *annual rate of profit*, which is different from the rate of profit. In an extreme example, if the turnover time for M–C(LP, MP)–P–C'–M' is 100 years, even a rate of profit of 100% should be meaningless, right?

$$\text{Annual rate of profit} = n \cdot S/(C+V) \text{ (n being annual turnover times)}$$

The formula for the annual rate of profit can be gotten by multiplying the rate of profit formula by n. And n refers to annual turnover times. As for Piece of Cake Bakery, which has shortened its turnover time to 6 months, has its annual turnover times n at 2. So, as we multiply its old rate of profit of 20% by 2, its annual turnover times, the company's annual rate of profit is 40%. As the turnover time is shortened by half, its annual rate of profit has doubled. If turnover time is shortened to 4 months, the annual number of capital turnover times is 3, so annual rate of profit is 60%.

As decreased turnover time increases the annual rate of profit, capitalists want to speed up production and sales. So, they run the factory 24/7 with two or three shifts, day and night.

There's one more reason for non-stop factory operation. It's the machines and facilities used in production. When new machines emerge through technological development, old machines and facilities become obsolete. If your competitors acquire new machines and facilities, outdated machines and facilities are bound to fall behind. And the capitalists have to make the most of their old machines and facilities before new machines and facilities show up. That way, they are more likely to recover the costs for buying machines and facilities.

Division of roles of capital and surplus value

A: So, shortening turnover time should matter as much for the circulation process as for production. Faster sales would mean faster recovery of funds.

Lecturer: That's right. It is as crucial for the circulation process as for the production process to shorten times. This refers to the C'–M' portion of the general formula for capital M–C(LP, MP)–P–C'–M'.

Let me put it this way. Piece of Cake Bakery has opened its stores in every area with a large population and is selling its products through them. One day, its CEO realizes that it is very inefficient for his company to sell products directly to end consumers. The costs for opening stores are pretty heavy, and the wages for the store staff are costly, too. The CEO of Piece of Cake Bakery now thinks it would be helpful in reducing costs and maximizing profits to entrust the sales of the company's products to a company that specializes in retail distribution.

Home Depot, Costco, and Walmart are big retail chains. These companies buy products at wholesale prices and sell them to consumers at retail prices. The difference between wholesale price and retail price generates their profits. Such companies decided to specialize in the portion of C'–M', out of M–C(LP, MP)–P–C'–M': different roles taken inside capital. Specialization with different assigned roles can generate profits more efficiently. So, when capital is used to specialize in distribution, as those companies do, it is called *commercial capital*. Meanwhile, those manufacturers like Piece of Cake Bakery are called *industrial capital*.

Student B: I thought that division of labor would happen only in production, but interestingly, it also happens with capital. Any other types of capital than industrial and commercial capital?

Lecturer: There is *finance capital* in addition to industrial and commercial capital. When you look at the general formula for capital M–C(LP, MP)–P–C'–M', you can see that it needs start-up capital M.

In general, a capitalist obtains his or her start-up capital not only with his on-hand cash but also by taking out a loan from the financial industry. That's because getting a loan and starting a bigger business is more advantageous than starting up on a small scale. Moreover, initial facility investment is on the increase owing to technological development.

The capital that lends funds and takes interests in exchange is called finance capital. Besides, there is landed capital. It leases land and collects a rent for it. Industrial capital, commercial capital, finance capital, and landed capital acquire profits while performing their given roles in the process of M–C(LP, MP)–P–C'–M'.

- Industrial capital: Makes profits by making goods and transferring them to commercial capital

- Commercial capital: takes profits by selling the goods to consumers

- Finance capital: takes profits by loaning out funds

- Landed capital: takes profits by leasing land

These all share the title of *capital*, but they really aren't the same. Why?

Student A: Manufacturers should want to sell their goods to distributors at higher wholesale prices, whereas distributors should want to buy them at cheaper prices. Isn't their conflict pretty natural? Newspapers are running stories about how mega stores are overusing their power over their suppliers. And about finance capital? Financial companies should want to get higher interests whereas companies that have to borrow reduce their interest cost by trying to get loans at lower interest rates. Landed capital should in turn pit themselves against their tenants over rents.

Lecturer: Correct. Yet, there's one thing that should never be overlooked. The profits for industrial capital, for commercial capital, for finance capital, and for landed capital all shared one and the same source. That's the surplus value taken away from workers. Different fractions of capital take certain roles out of M–C(LP, MP)–P–C'–M' and split up among them the surplus value created in production process by workers. You can easily understand this if you imagine one single pie cut in pieces and taken by several persons.

For this reason, different fractions of capital, which may be in conflict with one another, take the same stance toward workers. As long as the pie of surplus value gets bigger, different fractions of capital should get larger portions. When workers unite and demand their rights, these different fractions of capital instantly join in solidarity as a group of capitalists.

Student B: I have a question. This is all pretty novel and shocking stuff, which I find curious and fun. Frankly, however, I feel uncomfortable and confused. Marx seems to argue that because capitalism is wrong in many ways, we ultimately should go for socialism, communism, which is wrong in my opinion. While common ownership and management puts up a more egalitarian and democratic façade, I'm pretty sure that after all is said and done, nobody will take responsibility and everybody will try to stay in their comfort zone. Socialism too has failed. Meanwhile, capitalism has changed a lot.

I agree with the recent view that we need *capitalism with a human face*. I understand that capitalism exerts a bad influence on a society in many respects. It's obvious from the voice of self-reflection heard around the world. I think *sustainable capitalism* has come out of the search for alternatives. In my opinion, it's more realistic for capitalists to arm themselves with a sense of responsibility and ethical awareness in managing their companies. I too dream of running a company someday. And I want to try a management model that can set an example to others.

Lecturer: OK, I understand your unease. Lately, we see many news stories talking about *sustainable capitalism*. That's a wake-up call about capitalism, which is running wild. It should suggest that we need *good capitalists* who aren't focused on their personal interests alone but contribute to society.

As I said in our last lecture, however, with a *good* capitalist, a company is likelier to go belly up in the face of a withering competition in the market. When capitalists are educated people, how can they not know the importance of the environment and human rights? In real life, however, installing a wastewater purifying system and putting filters in smokestacks incurs extra costs, thus reducing profits. So, it'd be more profitable not to get a wastewater purifying system and to *grease the palms* of environmental officials instead. It's the same with the issue of part-time and temp workers. No capitalists would want to see their children work without benefits. Society-wide, however, everyone prefers to hire part-timers or temps to cut down on labor cost.

With individual companies left to their decisions, these problems are practically impossible to solve, because a company's primary goal is not the public good but the capitalist's private interests. The government should mobilize laws and systems for the public good. But if government takes regulatory measures, the big capitalists will furiously protest, saying that suppression of free market chills the economy.

Existence determines consciousness

Marx famously said, "Existence determines consciousness." To put this aphorism to the capitalist, it means that the mode of *existence* as a capitalist forms the *consciousness* of a capitalist. If you live the life of a capitalist whose ultimate goal is to pursue profits in the capitalist system, your consciousness will form in such a way that you'll exploit workers and overlook the preciousness of the environment, to survive in the structure.

Of course, this doesn't mean that *good* capitalists don't exist. Sometimes, good capitalists win market competition. However, such cases are pretty rare. Likewise, water flowing from higher to lower places doesn't necessarily mean that all water molecules move downward. Some water molecules *do* move upward when they clash with other molecules. But, can we say that water flows upward just because one single molecule moves back up for a second? A certain capitalist can be *good*, but the capitalist class in general cannot be *good* in the structure of capitalist competition.

In this context, I'm skeptical about *sustainable capitalism*. Of course, capitalist societies go through endless change and some countries do have a top-of-the-line welfare system. Strictly speaking, such a welfare system isn't a capitalist program. Rather, it is closer to the socialist program. If welfare is further expanded in the near future and the part of the economy that private business handles becomes larger than the part that the state and the community handle, such a society will no longer be entirely a capitalist society. It will mean a next level has been achieved.

Also, when we consider whether a capitalist is someone who can reform or change a capitalist society, the answer is negative, because the capitalist system is the *proprietor* of a capitalist society. Say, can a slave master change and reform a slave society? The capitalist class can maintain its power through the continuation of the capitalist society. For capitalists, now is the paradise. If you tell people who are in their prime, in paradise, that they should change the society because their good luck is wrong, would it make sense?

To the contrary, the working class carries on its shoulder the contradictions of the capitalist society. Workers have every reason to reform and change the capitalist society that is driving them to exploitation.

Workers are responsible for changing the world

Student B: I understand fairly well that the structure of a capitalist society imposes a tough life on workers. Wasn't it the same in the societies before capitalism? In the slave society, slaves were treated like animals. In the feudal society, serfs were subjected to exploitation, too. However, they couldn't change the world. Isn't the fate of workers similar to that of slaves or serfs? Am I too pessimistic?

Lecturer: In fact, nobody knows what the future will be like. But the working class differs from slaves or serfs in ancient days in one key respect. Slaves and serfs made the exploited class that bore the full brunt of the contradictions of their societies. But they had no *idea*. Humans view the world and perceive the problems through the prism of some idea. Since they had no idea with which they could make a critical analysis or judgment of the world, they didn't know what was wrong and what they should fix, even when they were being exploited. All they had was *en-soi* anger at a choking reality. Occasionally, their anger exploded into a massive revolt or uprising and they won some minor battles, but without an *idea* that could properly analyze the reality and provide solutions, they ended up defeated in a war.

The working class fundamentally differs from slaves or serfs in this respect. The working class has an idea. It is an idea that provides a scientific analysis of the capitalist society and precisely identifies its contradictions, thus telling people how to change the world. Karl Marx was a historical figure who broke the ground for the idea.

A capitalist society needs fairly well-educated workers to perform its tasks. So, it implements *general education* which provides a certain level of schooling for everyone. This gives workers an edge that slaves and serfs never had. Progressive intellectuals deliver the idea to the working class who have a certain level of education. *Enlightened* and with their consciousness elevated, the working class creates labor unions or a progressive party to run for election. The history of welfare states shows that their welfare was built when laws and systems were changed by a labor party, socialist party, or social democratic party that came to power.

Humans are not just passively influenced by a given environment and social structure. If existence had determined consciousness all the time, the history of humankind couldn't have made the progress that it has achieved. Humans are born for *action*. With our free hands, we can change our given environment.

Ideas and organization are basic conditions for action. An idea can set the direction for one's action, and an organization firmly united in pursuing one single idea can ensure powerful action. With ideas and organization, working people have the potential to change the world, unlike slaves or serfs. And the possibility is being demonstrated by several existing welfare states.

Student B: Now I've heard you speak, I'm afraid I overlooked that aspect. And we're studying *Das Kapital* by Marx to learn such ideas. I'm shocked to learn more about all this. Sometimes, I have this unbearable anger welling up.

Lecturer: Anger isn't always bad. Humans aren't robots, right? If humans have no feelings, we couldn't get angry at actual wrongs. You wouldn't find the will to get wrongs right. Anger at injustices is the driving power that changes the world. *Sensation* is as important as *reason*. While reason serves as our rudder, sensation is like driving force.

Student C: I think education is a serious problem now. Honestly, I've never learned this in school, from elementary school up to now. Since most of us are destined to be workers, our school education seems to show us the world viewed by capitalists instead of what workers need to know. School textbooks say that the invisible hand in the market makes harmonious decisions about everything. I've never learned anything that offers a serious reflection on why the issue of temp work has been created, why workers should always have a difficult life even when they work hard, or why the gap between rich and poor is widening this badly. My father worked harder than anyone else for the company. But he got laid off a long time ago. My mother is working part-time, as a cashier, for a mega store in our neighborhood. So far, my schools have never offered me a serious teaching about how a worker should live.

Lecturer: Indeed, education is a serious problem. It was worse when I was a student. Anything that explained or illustrated Communism was banned, and an *anti-Communist* theme was built into history and political books as a matter of course. It would be nice if schools gave fair treatment to both sides, but it's all tilted in favor of the capitalists. At least, schools should teach things like labor legislation. Students should know how to protect their rights as workers or they'll end up forfeiting income and benefits without even realizing it.

Today, I seem to have rambled a bit while trying to field your questions. In our next lecture, we'll discuss monopoly capital and economic crisis.

Points to Ponder

- Explain the concept of capital turnover time.
- Why is it that shorter capital turnover time benefits the capitalist?
- Characterize industrial capital, commercial capital, finance capital, and landed capital.
- What makes the working class the world changer?

Lecturer: We're already in our eleventh lecture. Time flies. Today, we're going to talk about monopoly capital and economic crisis. Before we start, let's go over what we have covered so far. Shall we write down the titles of our lectures to date?

Lecture 1 — Why Should We Study *Das Kapital*?

Lecture 2 — Capitalism Turns Everything into a Commodity

Lecture 3 — Money Has Turned into Capital

Lecture 4 — Profit Comes from Time Taken Away from Workers

Lecture 5 — Why Do Companies Like It If You Work Late?

Lecture 6 — Technological Development Furthers Exploitation

Lecture 7 — Performance-Related Pay? It Strengthens Self-Exploitation

Lecture 8 — Selfish People Are Molded to Fit a Capitalist Society

Lecture 9 — How Does a Capitalist Use Profit?

Lecture 10 — Capitalists Fight over Surplus Value

Now, when I get a book, I take a careful look at the table of contents. What is discussed in the book shows in the contents. If you have studied it right, you should be able to remember their details just by looking at the lecture titles. How about you?

Student A: In Lecture 3, you said that money and capital were two different things, which I couldn't figure out precisely. Until then I failed to grasp the meaning of the word *capital*. As I kept on studying, the concept became clearer and clearer. I also pictured in my head the image of capital whose size kept growing forever, by gobbling up workers' surplus value. Now, I clearly understand the statement that money functions as capital.

Student B: I was impressed by the talk of people cut out for capitalism in Lecture 8. Honestly, as I thought that humans are selfish by nature, I perhaps had no expectation of humans. I was kind of cynical and pessimistic. Now that we know the matrix that makes people selfish is the capitalist society, my view of life has totally changed.

The performance-related pay in Lecture 7 was surprising, too. Previously, I thought that performance-related pay was reasonable since you could get paid for your hard work. And the suggestion that capitalists could more efficiently exploit people through performance-related pay was, what should I say, quite an eye-opener.

Lecturer: You guys seem to have worked hard. As you all know, the essence is Lecture 4, which deals with *the theory of surplus value*, the heart of *Das Kapital* by Karl Marx. If you understand Lecture 4 rightly, you can logically get the other details without difficulty.

What we discuss in our lecture is a portion of *Das Kapital*. If this lecture piques your curiosity, please feel free to get your copy of the book and read the whole thing. Of course, it won't be easy with such tough content coming in a large volume, but my lecture should help you.

Monopoly capital, small and medium capital, and workers

Lecturer: Then, shall we go back to the salt mines? I said we were going to talk about monopoly capital and economic crises. You guys are familiar with *monopoly capital*, aren't you? It refers to big corporations that dominate their markets, like Samsung, Hyundai, Google, and Amazon. But, these companies weren't born as monopoly capital. They grew in size to become monopoly capital either by defeating other capitals in competition or by receiving politically preferential treatment. Marx came up with the concept of *concentration* to explain the formation of monopoly capital through market competition, and Lenin added the concept of centralization.

First, concentration. You remember learning the concept of expanded reproduction? Expanding production by purchasing extra means of production and labor power with earned profits was called expanded reproduction. If profits continue to be reinvested, a company will grow in size, won't it? The process in which capital size is increased through expanded reproduction is called concentration of capital.

Then, what is centralization of capital? In the market, a number of companies engage in no-holds-barred competition. Some companies are triumphantly increasing their size, while others fall behind and go out of business. And companies whose business get worse or face bankruptcy are taken over by other companies. Increasing the size of capital through merger and acquisition is called centralization of capital.

A company that has grown in size through concentration and centralization acquires such a huge influence that it obtains a monopolistic position. This is the growth of monopoly capital as explained by Marx.

Come to think of it, the emergence of monopoly capital in a capitalist society is inevitable. Let's say 100 bakeries nationwide are competing in the market. Is it possible for the companies to develop simultaneously at similar rates while keeping an appropriate balance in market share? Of course, it's impossible. When companies engage in life-and-death market competition, winner and loser will inevitably come out. The winner increases its market share endlessly by actively taking advantage of its favorable situation, from which process monopoly capital emerges.

Student A: I saw civic organizations hold a press conference in the news. They were arguing that monopoly corporations had to be dismantled, saying that fostering small and medium-sized enterprises (SMEs) would be an economic solution. While studying *Das Kapital*, I came to view economic phenomena from the viewpoint of workers, but aren't big corporation capitalists and SME capitalists the same to workers in that they exploit them?

Lecturer: It's not that simple. Monopoly capital's tyranny and harm to the market are just too huge to say that it's quite the same for big corporations and smaller businesses. It's close to impossible for smaller businesses to go *mano a mano* with giant monopolistic corporations in the market and defeat them. Many SMEs survive precisely by supplying parts or materials to big corporations. Some SMEs *do* scratch by in niche markets where big corporations aren't participating, though.

SMEs that do survive as suppliers to big corporations often suffer anyway, because big-time companies overuse their power by cutting back the price they're willing to pay for the goods supplied or by making late payments. However, the SMEs can't protest, because they'll go out of business if big corporations switch to other suppliers.

Even those SMEs that scratch by in niche markets experience the same anxiety. Exploring new turf in search of profits, big corporations often go into niche markets. Late-comers as they are, big corporations quickly overwhelm the old-timer SMEs in the market. Since subsidiaries of one big corporation frequently give contracts or provide unjustified support to one another, fair competition is out. A lot of SMEs are acquired by big corporations.

Consumers can't avoid the tyranny of big corporations, either. Free from competitors, monopoly capital has the huge power to control market prices. They can adjust their supply of products and they don't have to consider other companies in determining prices. Consumers have to buy products at higher prices if companies are no longer competing.

Trying to dismantle big corporations without much thought, just because monopolistic big companies have a lot of problems, can't be the best approach. Big monopolistic capitals have their merits. With their ample funds and enormous workforce, big corporations can develop technologies and undertake big projects, projects that the same SMEs can never carry out. And there are industries that big corporations alone can handle. They're industries that require huge facility investment and workforce such as semiconductor, auto, and shipbuilding. So, it would be narrow-minded to put all big corporations in a negative light and arguing for their dismantlement no matter what.

Nationalization and democratic operation of companies

Student A: Then, how should we approach the question of big corporations?

Lecturer: First of all, we shouldn't approach it so that big corporations are split while SMEs are enlarged. We should create an environment in which companies enjoy fair competition. And we should revamp the laws and systems lest big corporations tyrannize over SMEs by taking advantage of their dominant position. Let big corporations perform where their merits may find their best use. If this doesn't come to fruition and big corporations are dismantled and made available to potential buyers in the market, big foreign capitalists will buy them in all likelihood.

In fact, in the wake of the 1997 financial crisis that led to an IMF bailout, a considerable portion of the stocks of major Korean banks and companies was sold to foreign capital. Compared to domestic capital, foreign money is pretty insensitive to the public opinion and political atmosphere in South Korea. They don't have their base in Korea, and they only want to make money and leave. So, they execute more cold-hearted layoffs than Korean money, or frequently engage in abnormal operations of companies to raise the stock prices shortly. They frequently fail to re-invest profits but pocket them as their dividends. Some people say that capital has no nationality, but this shows that it has nationalities.

Marx believed that huge monopolistic companies should be nationalized. He thought that a company so powerful that it would exert society-wide influence should never be left in the hands of a certain person or several individuals. He said that such companies need democratic management, not in the interests of an individual but in the interests of the whole community.

Student C: I understand why Marx argued for nationalization, but honestly, that sounds unrealistic. Of course, corporate democracy would be nice. But nationalization transfers ownership from individuals to the state. Even though capital is created through exploitation of workers, just think how violently capitalists would react. I think it's out of the question.

Lecturer: Of course, there will be huge resistance. Nonetheless, there were cases in which industries with major society-wide influence were nationalized.

If you look into the shares of big corporations, individuals rarely own so many shares that they can hold sway over the companies. The ownership is distributed among a number of shareholders. Still, the bigger problem is that certain families hold sway over companies. As their shares are widespread, the state can exercise a greater-than-expected influence by getting some portion of a company's shares. Government funds such as National Pension Service already own not a small portion of shares of major companies. So, if only the government shows a stronger commitment, it will become possible to push for the nationalization of big corporations and intervene in their management for public benefits.

Anyway, there are conflicts and contradictions between monopoly capital and small and medium capital. That's because increased market domination by monopoly capital is likelier to drive small and medium capital out of the market. And such economic conflicts are reflected in politics. As a Presidential candidate, Barack Obama's campaign portrayed him as a friend of people like "Joe the Plumber." But it turns out that Obama was a protégé of the "megadonor" George Soros, an enormously powerful capitalist with his own agenda.

Politicians like this talk a lot during elections, but once they're in power, neither party could care less. They explain that increasing labor cost would be a drag on the economy. The two parties behave similarly for a reason. Big-corporation capitalists and SME capitalists alike prefer irregular employment.

With the progressive parties divided and registering low public ratings, they can't implement a policy that can solve the issue of irregular workers. Awakened workers should naturally support the progressive parties, but workers vote against their interests at every election owing to their conservative education and the conservative press. And miles to go before we sleep.

Student D: Frankly, I've always heard "nationalization" was not desirable and that privatization would be more progressive. Well, come to think of it, privatizing public corporations actually means putting public resources in the hands of capitalist companies that pursue profit. What about our water supply?

Are our municipal utilities provided through private companies?

Lecturer: We were talking about monopoly capital before we digressed into a talk of politics. Economy and politics are like the head and tail of a coin, and they're simply inseparable. OK, that's it for monopoly capital. Now, we talk about economic crisis.

What occurs to you when you hear the term, *economic crisis*?

Capitalism and economic crisis

Student E: That reminds me of the 1997 financial crisis. My father, who had his own business, had such a hard time that the company was inching close to bankruptcy. My sister was getting violin lessons to prepare for music college, but she seriously considered quitting. A music major is costly. Isn't that an economic crisis, an economy crashing all at once just like that?

Lecturer: Right. The 1997 financial crisis helps you see what an economic crisis is like. At that time, a great number of companies laid off their workers. Not a day passed but companies went out of business, while there were endless suicides out of despair at difficult livelihood. The Korean economy, which looked so rosy in the early 1990s, collapsed all at once, starting in late 1997.

Every capitalist society has this business cycle. An economy that enjoys ascendancy at one moment slips into a slump after a while. In general, an *economic crisis* refers to the point in time that an ascendant and climaxing economy abruptly crashes.

If you look at the history of humankind, economic crises were always out there, not only during the capitalist era. What kind of economic crises were there back when people lived by farming and depended entirely on the power of humans and cattle?

Student A: Maybe they were natural disasters?

Lecturer: Right. When disasters like drought or flood ruined crops, severe food shortage set in, causing massive starvation through lack of food. If you browse *Samguksagi* (The Chronicles of the Three States), you often run into records about starvation from food crises. In those days, economic crises were brought about by absolute shortage of materials for daily living.

But the economic crises in capitalism are quite different from those economic crises. They are crises of supra-production as opposed to shortages. Did people suffer from an absolute food shortage during the financial crisis in 1997? Korean companies had huge stockpiles of goods in their warehouses. The problem is that there were more goods on hand than could be sold in a timely manner. And people committed suicide out of despair at their difficult life. While companies go out of business with their warehouses overflowing with goods, people experience utter desolation because they can't provide for their daily life. This extreme contradiction characterizes the economic crises in capitalism. That shatters the myth of mainstream economics that argues that supply and demand are appropriately adjusted by the invisible hand in the market.

Student A: Yes, that's quite different. I read in a book that the modern-day productive forces have reached such a level that we have more than enough food for the entire world population. But countless people still die of starvation, so something's definitely wrong with the social system. But what makes an economic crisis happen, when we aren't running out of supplies?

Lecturer: A capitalist society always overflows with goods. The point is that when a crisis kicks off, that overflow of goods doesn't sell well. If goods don't sell, what happens to companies? When they have to pay interests for loans and honor the promissory notes issued for purchased materials, products aren't selling, so they have a large stock in warehouses and are broke. They don't have enough money for their workers' salaries. Noticing the financial squeeze of the companies, their banks heap pressure on them to recover some of the loans before late.

If things get tight for companies, banks get in trouble, too. If they lose interest revenue and can't collect the principal of loans from companies, the financial condition will get worse for the banks. So, banks tighten loan review and try to collect the principal of any potentially delinquent loans. As a result, a credit crunch occurs, making it hard to find willing lenders of money. Lenders are only willing to lend for a high rate of interest.

Interest is the price of money, and with money supply drastically dwindling, interest rates soar according to the law of supply and demand. If interest rates go up, the interest burden increases for households and companies that borrowed money at variable interest rates. And anyone who can't handle increased interest rates also go belly up. With companies going bankrupt, banks are increasingly insolvent, and in the worst-case scenario, even banks go bust. In a crisis, the economy plummets into a bottomless pit.

I've given you a summary of how a crisis unfolds. Here, the really important moment is when a crisis starts. Companies begin to see their goods pile up in warehouses due to poor sales from a certain moment, which is the start of a crisis.

Then, why is it that products don't sell and stock piles up in warehouses *from a certain moment*? Marx ascribes it to *the anarchy of production* that characterizes the capitalist society. What is this concept of anarchy of production all about? Let's take a look.

Capitalists produce and sell goods solely in pursuit of profits. With business ticking up, capitalists bet on the rosy prospects and increase production while making new investments. And banks increase loans expecting interest revenue. They should *strike while the iron is hot*, right? A series of processes create a synergy and send business in an ascending ride, thus starting a *boom*. With a boom lasting until business heats up, the economy is now into overproduction.

Overproduction doesn't just mean that too many goods have been produced. What it means is that they have produced too many goods to be consumed with the purchasing power of consumers. With a well-developed credit system available now, people can take out a loan to invest and spend even if they have no money right now. This is how a bubble forms in an economy.

Regrettably enough, a bubble cannot last. Bubbles will eventually burst. As companies have stock pile up in warehouses, they can't even recover the costs for making products. And their profit margin drops. To make a long story short, *overproduction* refers to the condition in which too many goods have been produced for capitalists to pursue any normal profits.

In a capitalist society, the decision about production is entirely up to the capitalist. Marx described this peculiarity as anarchy of production. If an economy can be controlled by the whole society, a bubble can be prevented by adjusting the production of different companies. But in a capitalist society, this is regarded as unjustified intervention in the management of individual companies. In Marx's view, the anarchy of production begets overproduction, which causes periodic economic crises.

Dramatic moments of the capitalist contradictions

Student B: When a crisis is caused by the capitalist's decision to create overproduction, aren't workers the greatest victims? Countless workers get laid off and their families break up and people even take their own life. While capitalists too sustain damage, that won't compare to the difficulties experienced by workers.

Lecturer: I think an economic crisis is the phase that demonstrates the contradiction of capitalism most violently and obviously. Even if a crisis sets in, the financial hardships wouldn't be so severe if the goods piled up in the warehouses were shared with the working class to meet their daily needs. They can't be sold anyway. And in fact, the goods that pile up in the warehouses were made by workers.

However, such acts constitute a breach of private property, the inviolable sanctuary of the capitalist society. What if, during the last financial crisis, people had stormed the warehouses yelling "our livelihood comes first!"? Chances are, they all would have been branded as rioters and gotten locked up.

The development of financial techniques not only prods economic crises but spreads them around the world. With financial products traded real time through the internet, huge amounts of money instantly cross borders. In a short period of time, big bubbles can be created. Furthermore, *asset-backed securities* created from fragmented fixed assets like real estate are sold across borders. If these financial products go bad all at once, the world economy could fall into a bottomless pit. The 2007 global crisis that followed the U.S. sub-prime mortgage crisis clearly demonstrated such a hazard.

A capitalist economy characteristically repeats ups and downs in business cycle periodically. While there are different opinions on whether the period is 10 or 20 years or if it follows an irregular pattern, it is doubtless that economic crises have registered periodicity since the establishment of the capitalist system.

One more thing that needs to be considered in analyzing

economic crises is *underconsumption*. Insufficient purchasing power of consumers can make a stock pile up in a company's warehouses, right? What would happen if the explosive increase of irregular workers continues as now? Irregular workers get half the income of regular workers, so they have less purchasing power. If irregular workers increase, a society's purchasing power sharply diminishes. Capitalists prefer irregular workers, but they dig their own graves by doing so. It's because most of the buyers of their goods are actually workers.

Student A: Drastically increasing irregular workers for greater profits can ultimately trigger underconsumption for the whole society and make the economy get worse. It's crazy that capitalists prefer irregular workers in such a stark reality.

Student B: So far, I thought that economic crises happen because of government intervention in markets. I learned that economic crises occur from a disturbed market mechanism because the government frequently intervenes instead of leaving it up to the market. But according to Marx, even if the capitalist market economy properly functions, economic crises will inevitably and periodically occur because of its anarchic character. Is it why Marx came up with *a planned economy* as a solution?

Lecturer: Correct. Marx thought that an economy should not be run in an anarchic fashion according to the capitalists' personal desire to pursue profits, but that the economy should be operated in a democratic and *planned* manner by jointly managing means of production. He thought, that would steer clear of the odd phenomenon of economic crisis.

Meanwhile, economic crises also mean new opportunities to some capitalists. Companies that survive a crisis acquire endangered or bankrupt companies at a fire-sale price. By increasing their size further, they grow into monopoly capital. Also, they introduce new production technology to get through a difficult situation. In good times, they don't feel the need to make changes, but in a crisis, they implement changes. I said that labor unions generally have objections to introducing new production technology. It's because it could reduce their jobs. In a crisis, the power of labor unions get weakened by layoffs and restructuring. So, capitalists face less stiff resistance in introducing new technology.

When a crisis strikes, countless people get laid off in the name of restructuring, unleashing a huge reserve army of labor, that is, jobless people including youths who can't find jobs. The mainstream economics *assumes* that employment and unemployment depend on a worker's choice, which is outrageous. They can't get a job because no company is hiring even if they want to work. Capitalists don't hire workers, unless they're convinced that they can make money by hiring more workers. Capitalists aren't social workers. And in an economic crisis when the economy is crumbling, what profits could they expect in hiring workers? They're just busy firing them.

It isn't because workers avoid 3D occupations or there is too large a population for an industry that the capitalist society has a large reserve army of labor. It's because the available population is larger than what the capitalists need to maintain their production while earning appropriate profits. As I mentioned in my last Thomas Robert Malthus lecture, people who aren't helpful in creating the capitalist's profit are predestined to live jobless. You may have heard of a sociologist named Thomas Robert Malthus (1766-1834). He was the man who fascinated the world with his unique *Principle of Population* which stated that the world would face a crisis as human population registers exponential growth whereas food registers arithmetic growth. Modern world enjoys affluence. It has productive forces that can feed the entire world population. Nevertheless, only a few people are well-to-do where as a great majority of people are poor. This reality cannot be explained with the Malthusian principle of population. The capitalist principle of population focuses on whether it helps capital create profits or not.

Student A: It's sad that the fate of workers should be decided by whether a capitalist pursues profit or not. And those who don't help capital create profits are *superfluous people*, unnecessary leftover people....

Lecturer: That's the regrettable reality of life. According to Marxist theory, the fundamental cause of a crisis is capitalism *itself*. And this is the condition in which the sole objective of production is profit-taking and in which what to produce in what quantity is determined by the capitalist's desire to pursue profit. Economic crises have shown that the capitalist economy has no ability to harmonize production and consumption for the whole society. Uncontrolled pursuit of profit and uncontrolled production, that is, the anarchy of production has opened the door to crises. An economic crisis represents the moment that reveals the contradiction of capitalism with destructive results and enormous losses.

Today, we have discussed the topic of monopoly capital and economic crisis. While it feels somewhat insufficient, we'll leave it at that. After all, there's only solitary road to learning. If you're interested, please find more books and do more study.

Points to Ponder

- Explain the concentration and centralization of capital.
- In what respect do the economic crises in capitalism differ from the economic crises in the previous time periods?
- Describe the meaning of overproduction.
- What does anarchy of production mean?
- Compare the principle of population by Malthus and the capitalist principle of population by Marx.

LECTURE 12 — RATE OF PROFIT TENDS TO FALL

Lecturer: Today, we're going to study *the tendency of the rate of profit to fall*, which is one of the most contentious topics in *Das Kapital*. As it's going to be a little bit more difficult compared to what we have covered so far, please stay put. Since it is about the tendency of the rate of profit to fall, let me begin with the rate of profit.

Rate of profit = $S/(C+V)$

In this formula, we divide both denominator and numerator by V to get the following result.

Rate of profit = $S/(C+V)$ = $(S/V)/((C+V)/V)$ = $(S/V)/(C/V+1)$ = (Rate of exploitation)/(Organic composition of capital+1)

S/V in the numerator is the *rate of exploitation.* C/V in the denominator refers to the organic composition of capital. In an earlier lecture, we studied the rate of exploitation and the organic composition of capital, right? If you're not so sure, repeat that part. Rising organic composition of capital means that the value of C/V, the organic composition of capital, increases. This is because from technological development, more money is needed to purchase constant capital C than variable capital V. Although we covered this before, we'll give it another look just to make sure.

Improved productivity brings rate of profit down

When investing $10 million in a business project, if you spend $2 million as constant capital C and $8 million as variable capital V, the organic composition of capital is as follows.

Organic composition of capital = C/V = 20/80 = 1/4 = 0.25

Lecturer: Technological development has led to the invention of a new machine. The machine handles what a number of workers used to do. So, when you invest $10 million, $8 million is spent as constant capital C and $2 million is spent as variable capital V. In the changed situation, the organic composition of capital is calculated as follows.

Organic composition of capital = C/V = 80/20 = 4/1 = 4

You can see that the organic composition of capital has increased from 0.25 to 4. In a capitalist society, what used to be done by humans tends to be done by machines, owing to technological development. So, C/V rises continuously. Let's suppose that in the rate of profit formula, the rate of exploitation S/V, the numerator, doesn't change much. If the denominator C/V continues to increase while the numerator value remains the same, the rate of profit tends to fall. This is called *the tendency of the rate of profit to fall due to the rising organic composition of capital*. The name is pretty long, isn't it?

Student A: Technological development in a capitalist society leads the rate of profit to fall in the long run, doesn't it? If the rate of profit falls continuously, the capitalist system registers no further growth and inevitably faces bankruptcy. Then, does the tendency of the rate of profit to fall predict a necessary end of capitalism? Because no profit is created in a society that aims at profit...

An increased exploitation ratio offsets a decreased rate of profit

Lecturer: Since that sensitive conclusion is drawn, the tendency of the rate of profit to fall due to the rising organic composition of capital constitutes a major controversy in Marx's book. Think about it, and you'll see that the rising organic composition of capital just logically leads the rate of profit to fall. The theoretical framework of *Das Kapital* supposes that profit derives from the time that is taken away from workers. So, fewer and fewer hired workers should mean less and less time that may be taken away from them, right?

Student A: The calculation assumes that the rate of exploitation in the numerator doesn't change much, but is it true? If this assumption is wrong, wouldn't the situation change?

Lecturer: That's a sharp question. In fact, *the tendency of the rate of profit to fall* is controversial, because both the factor that reduces the rate of profit and the factor that raises the rate of profit exist at the same time. Let me copy the rate of profit formula once again.

Rate of profit = $S/(C+V)$ = $(S/V)/(C/V+1)$

The rate of exploitation S/V in the numerator refers to the ratio of surplus labor against necessary labor. Earlier on, we assumed that there would be no big change in the rate of exploitation, but with technological development, the rate of exploitation tends to increase. You remember what you learned about relative surplus value, don't you? When the company acquired a new bread machine, the exchange value of 1 loaf of bread diminished from 3 labor hours to 2.5 labor hours. We'll calculate how the rate of exploitation changes before and after the introduction of the new machine, when daily working time is the same 8 hours and daily pay is the same 1 loaf of bread.

Before acquisition of new machine
8 labor hours = necessary labor (3 labor hours)+surplus labor (5 labor hours)
After acquisition of new machine
8 labor hours = necessary labor (2.5 labor hours)+surplus la-

bor 5.5 labor hours)

Before acquisition of new machine

$$S/V = 5/3 \approx 1.6$$

After acquisition of new machine

$$S/V = 5.5/2.5 = 2.2$$

With the acquisition of a new machine, the rate of exploitation increases. We see here that technological development tends to not only increase the organic composition of capital in the denominator but also to increase the rate of exploitation in the numerator.

Rate of profit falls in the long term

Student A: If both the denominator and numerator increase due to technological development, isn't it far-fetched to assume a long-term fall in the rate of profit?

Lecturer: That's right. If the organic composition of capital and the rate of exploitation increase simultaneously due to technological development, the outcome will depend on which increases faster. Now we're at this, shall we calculate the change in the rate of profit before and after the acquisition of the new bread machine? We'll get the same formula we used when studying relative surplus value.

[Formula 1] Exchange value of 8 loaves of bread = 8kg of flour (8 labor hours)+depreciation of bread machine (8 labor hours)+worker's 8 labor hours (8 labor hours) = 24 labor hours

[Formula 2] Exchange value of 16 loaves of bread = 16kg of flour (16 labor hours)+depreciation of bread machine (16 labor hours)+worker's 8 labor hours (8 labor hours) = 40 labor hours

[Formula 1] represents the condition before the acquisition of a new machine, while [Formula 2] shows the situation after.

Before the new machine was brought in, they produced 1 loaf of bread per hour, but after the machine was acquired, they came to produce 2 loaves of bread per hour. Now, let's calculate the rate of profit in the respective conditions (as in our earlier calculation, we now assume for convenience's sake that the bread machine too is consumable just like flour). To begin with, we reorganize each formula with C, V, and S to facilitate our calculation.

[Formula 3] Exchange value of 8 loaves of bread = C(16 labor hours)+V(3 labor hours)+S(5 labor hours) = 24 labor hours
[Formula 4] Exchange value of 16 loaves of bread = C(32 labor hours)+V(2.5 labor hours)+S(5.5 labor hours) = 40 labor hours

If you have faithfully followed the lecture, I'm sure you can understand this formula without my explanation. Those of you who have difficulty understanding this, please go back to check relative surplus value.

By putting specific numbers in the formula, we can get the following calculation.

Rate of profit before acquition of new machine = S/(C+V) = 5/(16+3)≃0.263

Rate of profit after acquisition of new machine = S/(C+V) = 5.5/(32+2.5)≃0.159

Student A: The rate of profit went down, indeed! In this case, the rising organic composition of capital has overwhelmed the rising rate of exploitation.

Lecturer: That's right! Marx thought that the rising organic composition of capital would surpass the rising rate of exploitation in the long run. So, he thought that the rate of profit would drop in the long run. If you look at the progress of capitalism, commodities that never existed before, like smartphones, emerge. Water was never traded as a commodity, but now we buy drinking water. As new commodities generally get high rates of profit, this works to offset the tendency of rate of profit to fall.

Anyway, the rate of profit formula incorporates both possibilities of rise and fall. It has motivated fierce debates. Some scholars try to prove the tendency of the rate of profit to fall by empirically calculating the long-term rate of profit while others want to negate it in the same method.

Student B: If so, if capitalism develops ever newer products and expands the areas for creating profits, it could offset the tendency of rate of profit to fall?

Lecturer: But, as capital expands its areas for creating profits, more and more people will suffer losses at the hands of capital. For example, what if they push for privatization of healthcare and the water supply until they completely commoditize both services? Then, poor people will be excluded from the services, right? And the society will grow more unstable. As capitalism extends its control, its damage increases. We need to remember that as well.

Student A: To me, the match between go player Lee Sedol and AlphaGo, the AI computer program, was quite impressive. They say there is even an AI that writes fiction. I was afraid that in the near future, robots would take over most of the human jobs. What's going to happen to capitalism when technological development enables robots to replace humans ...?

Lecturer: I get that question once in a while. Marxist theory says that the capitalist's profit comes from the surplus value created by workers in the production process. A logical conclusion is that if robots replace all human workers, no surplus value will be created. Because profit comes only out of time taken away from workers.

But, if technology develops to such an extent that robots that feel and think just like humans are employed in labor, would humans exploit robots? Could we say that humans extract surplus value from robots? We can't reach easy conclusions on the question. If robots get to completely supplant humans in work places, then we'll need some other social system than capitalism. In the capitalist system, a majority of people work and live off their wages. So, if robots replace humans in jobs, people will be starving because they can't collect their salaries. And if the current capitalist system persists in that situation, humans will face extinction.

Student B: Then, it will have to be either socialism or communism to ensure the survival of humankind.

Lecturer: Haha, that's what it looks like! Now, today's a beautiful day and we should wrap up class a little bit early. Everybody should get out and enjoy the sun.

Points to Ponder:

- Describe the relationship between organic composition of capital and rate profit.

- How come the tendency of rate of profit to fall can be a huge problem to a capitalist society?

- How does increasing rate of exploitation offset the tendency of rate of profit to fall?

- How do new commodities offset the tendency of rate of profit to fall?

LECTURE 13 — IMPERIALISM, THE MONSTER BEGOTTEN BY MONOPOLY CAPITAL

Lecture: I have good news for you. From here on, you won't see any more mathematical calculations.

Student C: Wow, that's good to hear.

Student A: Actually, the formulas presented such a clear formulation of the structure of capitalism that they piqued my curiosity. It's like watching the laws of the Newtonian physics.

Lecturer: Well, the attraction of science lies in discovering *laws* that pervade the whole world, in complexity and diversity. Newton was great because he discovered the *laws* that govern the motion of things and rendered them in the universal language of mathematics. In this sense, Marx was Newton of social sciences.

Student A: I got the same feeling. I found many things hard to understand about capitalist society. Why are there still so many poor people when people work so hard? Why is everything centered on money? And by reading *Das Kapital*, many of my longstanding questions have been solved. Now, I guess I know why they call Marx a genius.

Lecturer: I was floored when I first read *Das Kapital* as a college student. I wonder if the shock was similar to what people felt when they first heard that the earth was not the center of universe.

Now, we're going to talk about *imperialism*. What does the word *imperialism* make you think of?

Student A: I think of America. The country invaded Afghanistan, Iraq and so on and mistreated and killed a lot of civilians, as has been exposed by news media. They were all wars provoked for natural resources like gas and oil. The US built its embassy as large as Vatican City in Iraq. If I were an Iraqi national, what would I think, looking at the gigantic US embassy...?

Student B: When a powerful country invades, occupies, and rules a small and weak country, don't we call it imperialism? History has had several empires, such as the Roman Empire, the Ottoman Empire, the Spanish Empire, and the British Empire.

America as the leading imperialist country and monopoly capital

Lecturer: I think you guys have more or less the same understanding of imperialism. Now, let me ask you something. Why on earth do these *empires* invade and rule other countries?

Student A: Certainly for money, right? It is now public knowledge that when the US invaded Iraq, oil money had lobbied for it behind the scenes. I read a book titled *Rogue States Gone Mano a Mano with America*, which relates an episode on how an American company called United Fruit Company overthrew the progressive regime in Guatemala. The reason cited is that the Jacobo Árbenz government had breached the American fruit company's interests.

Student B: Apart from economic interest, they're probably more motivated by the need to maintain and increase their influence in other regions. Look, the United States sends its military troops to every corner of the planet. With their overwhelming military power, they browbeat countries all around the world. US forces are still in Germany and other parts of Europe since World War II, in South Korea, and in Japan.

Student C: As I understand, half of the shares of South Korean banks are owned by foreign capital, with a major portion of it coming from the US. When Lone Star Funds, the speculative capital, which took over Korea Exchange Bank at a fire-sale price, laid off a large number of workers to boost its stock price, and sold it off to pocket several billion dollars, I thought it was just too much. While several billion dollars was unlawfully transferred to an American speculative capital, the Korean government remained practically irrelevant, nervously peeking at what the US was at.

Lecturer: To my surprise, you guys are pretty knowledgeable about current affairs. What on earth gives rise to imperialist countries like America? As you just said, *money making*, that is, greed for profit lurks behind all this.

The US invaded Iraq and Afghanistan out of greed for natural resources like oil. Through Iraq War and Afghanistan War, the US military capitalists made huge money while clearing out their old inventory. US construction companies made lots of money in constructing new building in the land scorched by the US military forces. Even before 9/11, US government figures and representatives of the capitalists were meeting to discuss how to cut the pie up once the country invaded Iraq. It came as no surprise, because President George W. Bush and Vice President Dick Cheney were CEOs of oil company or arms manufacturers.

To understand the phenomenon of imperialism, we need to study monopoly capital. Once it dominates its home country, a monopoly capital feels itself cramped in the domestic market. To make more money, they will turn their eyes abroad. They find huge untapped markets beyond their borders. The governments of imperialist nations mobilize their military forces to force open the doors of the countries that their monopoly capitals are salivating at. They take those countries as their colonies. The imperialist monopoly capitals take advantage of the cheap raw materials and labor costs in the colonies and rack up enormous surplus profits by manufacturing industrial products at very low costs and reselling them in the colonies.

But, should we call this mode *classical imperialism*? As the method was adopted by the US for Iraq and Afghanistan, it may not be appropriate to describe it as classical. However, invasion with military power provokes the resistance of people in the colonies. Stiffer resistance incurs huge costs in managing and maintaining the colonies. In the worst-case scenario, they could lose their colonies. When the people of the colonies show intensified resistance and struggle, imperialism adopts some other response. Shall we call it *an astute imperialism*?

Neocolonialism, the astute imperialist policy of America

Student A: Isn't that the astute type of rule called *neocolonialism*?

Lecturer: That's right. A forceful rule that mobilizes military forces is colonialism, whereas a rule disguised in economic and cultural domination is called neocolonialism. People have used the term *neo-liberalism* for a while, and America's neocolonialist rule lurks behind the neo-liberalist scheme. Let me be specific about this.

You must have heard the names like WTO, IMF, and FTA quite a lot. WTO is the acronym of the World Trade Organization. The IMF is the International Monetary Fund. And FTA stands for the Free Trade Agreement. Behind these various and seemingly unrelated entities lies the neocolonialist intention of the United States.

The WTO had 164 member states in 2018. If you hear what the member countries discuss at their gatherings, it's about eliminating trade barriers. Some people may wonder what's so wrong with arguing for free, barrierless trade, but think again. Isn't this something that you've heard somewhere before? In the years of *military* imperialism, they arrived with troops in ironclad ships, and what did they say? They demanded the opening of ports for trade. Don't you see any similarity between the two? Today, countries support some of their industries with subsidies while imposing tariffs on imports. This is how they protect their fledgling industries until they stand own their own two feet. Most advanced countries grew in their early days. So, what's going to happen if every country flings open the doors of their markets? Weak economies could lose what foundation they may have laid so far. Naturally, imperialist monopoly capital would like to eliminate trade barriers promptly. Behind the WTO lies the desire of imperialist monopoly capital to pursue profit beyond national borders.

Anyway, the WTO has 164 countries at its meetings, so its discussions can't be easy. Since the countries come with all different interests, they more often than not sharply clash with one another, thus reaching a consensus only arduously. Even when an agreement is reached, it isn't very binding. The Free

Trade Agreement was the card that the US produced to end the gridlock.

Student A: I didn't know that was in the background. South Korea also got a Free Trade Agreement with the US, and detailed reports started a controversy by revealing that the agreement included many provisions that undermined our national sovereignty.

Lecturer: When the framework of the WTO didn't work for them, America switched its strategy to *defeat* in detail. Apart from the framework of the WTO, they picked out countries that speak the same economic language. An outstanding instance is NAFTA (North America Free Trade Agreement) that America signed with Canada and Mexico. And there's the Korea-US Free Trade Agreement.

Free Trade Agreements purport to be trade agreements concluded between two nations or among several nations through mutual negotiations, but if you look at the specifics, they include so many poison pills that they may be safely described as representing the surrender of economic sovereignty. Those countries which have entered into a Free Trade Agreement with the US are equally under her strong influence. By opening the doors of the partner country's market through a Free Trade Agreement, the United States facilitates the brisk advancement of its monopoly capital into the target country.

Student B: Now I see why the WTO and Free Trade Agreements are tools of neocolonialism. But the IMF sounds a little awkward, doesn't it? Doesn't the IMF just lend dollars to those countries mired in a currency crisis? I don't think it has anything to do with imperialism.

Lecturer: That's not true. After the Second World War, the US dollar came to be used as a reserve currency for international transactions (key currency), and countries had to have US dollars in their reserves to trade with other countries. Still, there are always countries that suffer from a shortage of dollars due to a trade deficit and so on. So, they created the IMF to provide emergency loans to countries that ran out of dollars. But countries that want to borrow dollars from the IMF have to accept whatever conditions the IMF imposes. And if you scrutinize those policies, you can see the true face of the IMF.

When our country nearly ran out of foreign reserves in the 1997 financial crisis, we had no choice but to seek emergency loans from the IMF. The IMF doesn't offer a lump-sum loan. They offered a loan split into several smaller sums with requirements as follows.

- Privatizing state corporations
- Eliminating government regulations
- Sharply reducing public spending in welfare, etc.
- Freezing and cutting down on wages
- Providing foreigners with a full access to local stock market
- Tax exemption or reduction for companies
- Neutering labor unions
- Implementing "flexible" labor policies such as introducing a layoff system

The IMF is a mechanism for imperialist incursions

Student C: And these clauses undermine our ability to manage our own economy; it's a form of imperialism, is that it?

Lecturer: That's right. They're policies that create an optimized local environment in which imperialist monopoly capital pursues profit. Once they've been privatized, big corporations are bought up and concentrated in fewer and fewer hands, whether those of Korean capitalists or of imperialist monopoly capital. Dismantling government regulations is about removing laws or systems that serve as stumbling blocks to pursuit of profit. If a layoff system and flexible labor market are established, they will generate a large number of unemployed people, right? Like the United States, Korea has seen a huge increase in temp assignments and part-time jobs, with a lower proportion of employees covered by what used to be normal benefits and protections. The IMF pushes such demands.

Furthermore, the IMF enforces high interest rates and currency depreciation, policies that secretly serve the interests of the imperialist and speculative financial capital. When our country was subjected to an IMF bailout, interest rates for bank deposits were running up to 20 percent. If interest rates are raised, foreign capital will flow in and increase the local foreign reserves that have been running out.

Now, let me explain currency depreciation. The exchange rate, which was 800 won for 1 US dollar before the financial crisis, rose to 1,600 won after the crisis. It was because of the depreciation implemented by the IMF, which was intended to get more dollars by increasing exports. If a company exports a product priced at 800 won, its export price is 1 dollar (at the exchange rate of 800 won to 1 dollar). If the exchange rate hikes to 1,600 won for 1 dollar, the export price drops by 50 cents. With the dollar price dropping, the product becomes more price competitive in foreign markets, which increases exports and then increases the country's foreign reserves with more dollars raked in as export prices.

But that's not the real reason for implementing a policy of high interest rates and currency depreciation. Those two policies work like a magic wand for speculative financial capitals seeking capital gains, and here's why. When South Korea received a bailout from the IMF, South Korean stock prices hit bottom, reflecting the difficult economy. With the IMF enforcing a policy of high interest rates, the local banks' interest rates soared close to 20 percent. What would you do under such circumstances? You just have to quickly get your money out of the stock market and put it into a bank. If everybody takes their money out of the stock market and sticks it in the bank, stock prices will crash through the floor into the basement.

It is then that the imperialist and speculative financial capital steps in. The IMF has already liberalized the local stock market, so the speculative capital faces no restrictions. Naturally, they sweep up potential blue chips whose prices have suffered a drastic fall.

At that time, over half of the country's bank shares fell into foreign hands. For example, more than two thirds of the shares of Kookmin Bank came to be owned by foreigners. Currency depreciation greatly contributes to this. Let's say, speculative financial capital has invested 1 million dollars in the stock market.

When 1 dollar is 800 won, you get 800 million won in exchange for 1 million dollars. You get twice that amount, however, if the exchange rate doubles. Thanks to currency depreciation, foreigners can buy twice as much stock. In a nutshell, a policy of high interest rates kills stock prices while currency depreciation increases the volume of stocks they can buy.

Student C: Well, that's astonishing! Thanks to the IMF's policies, foreign speculative financial capital was cleaning up, in a fire sale. That's pretty shocking.

Lecturer: What follows afterwards is no less important. With business recovering bit by bit, stock prices will recover slowly. And the IMF normalizes the interest rates that they raised. Then, what's going to happen? When interest rates go down, stock prices go up. So, money drawn out of banks moves to the stock market. With the money inflow, stock prices go further up. Imperialist, speculative financial capital, which acquired stocks at give-away prices, now gets a huge capital gain from the soaring stock prices.

As business recovers, the depreciated currency normalizes, too, which is again a boon to the financial capital. Let's say that the financial capital owns 1.6 billion-won-worth stocks. The dollar value of stocks matters more than their won value to the imperialist financial capital. That's because they evaluate their assets in dollar terms. When the exchange rate is 1,600 won for 1 dollar, 1.6 billion won is 1 million dollars. When the economy recovers and the currency exchange recovers its original rate of 800 won for 1 dollar, 1.6 billion won becomes 2 million dollars. The dollar value of stocks doubles just because the exchange rate falls.

To make a long story short, imperialist financial capital acquires the stocks of the companies at rock-bottom prices, riding on the IMF's policy of high interest rates and currency depreciation, and reaps enormous capital gains when the interest rates and currency exchange rate recover. Isn't it a piece of cake to make money? To make matters worse, speculative financial capital, which is interested more in maximizing short-term profits than in long-term investments, just unscrupulously creates stumbling blocks to the development of companies, such as massive layoffs or huge dividend payouts.

Student A: I can recall how Lone Star Funds, the speculative capital investment firm which took over Korea Exchange Bank, carried out massive layoffs and ran away with huge dividends and capital gain. As the company collected a profit of several billion dollars, it reportedly committed illegalities just brazenly. Meanwhile, the government couldn't respond properly....

Lecturer: Well over a hundred countries have been subjected to such measures by the IMF. The collapse of the economies in South and Central America in the 1980s was not unrelated to the IMF bailouts that concentrated in the regions. Thus, the IMF was the preacher of neo-liberalism.

Student B: If the IMF has so many member countries, how can the United States set all the rules?

Lecturer: The decision-making structure of the IMF is quite interesting. Its resolution is reached not with one vote for each country but one vote for every dollar invested. So, your voting right is in proportion to the amount of money you have invested in the IMF. Uniquely, a proposal requires a minimum 85% "yea" vote to pass, and the United States has 16.66% of the voting shares. When the US opposes a proposal, it cannot pass because the yea vote can never make the minimum 85%. Since Western countries close to America also have large portions, the IMF operation usually follows a line that benefits the US and other Western countries. For this reason, most of the member countries strive not to take a bailout from the IMF, even if they face severe financial crises.

South Korea too tried to cope with the financial crisis without a bailout from the IMF. It sought help from Japan, which was amenable to the idea. But the United States put strong pressure on Japan to keep them from intervening, so South Korea had no option but to get a bailout from the IMF. That way, the Americans could reap the greatest benefits.

Student C: It's a terrifying world. You're saying that neo-liberalist globalization is deeply imbued with speculative financial capital's greed... I'm dumbfounded.

Lecturer: I understand that. So was I. As you can see from what I've related so far, behind imperialism lies the desire of monopoly capital to pursue profit. Just as the appearance of monopoly capital is inevitable in the capitalist society, the unequal development of capitalism among different countries perhaps makes the emergence of imperialist nations inevitable. Unless people have a clear understanding of this situation and unless small countries register a well-orchestrated response against imperialism, world powers won't stop their imperialist tyranny.

Points to Ponder

- Why do some people call the United States an imperialist nation?

- Let's consider imperialism and the desire of monopoly capital.

- Why is neo-liberalism the imperialist policy of the United States?

Lecture 14 — The State Is Anything but Neutral

Lecturer: We've made it to my last lecture. Today, we're talking about the *government*. The state is a broad and profound topic. A proper discussion could take one whole semester. So, in this lecture, I'll go over the character and meaning of the state as far as it is related to capitalism. When you hear the word "government," what does it bring to mind?

Student D: Elections! Honestly, I don't have much faith in elections. I see politicians who ordinarily look down on people but beg for votes during elections. Then they don't keep their word, anyway.

Student A: While politicians are to blame for some wrongs, the state *does* work for public security and protect people's properties, doesn't it? I'm a police administration major. Not necessarily because of my major, people can have a safer life because state is in charge of public security.

Student B: When it comes to the state, I get to think of *law* first. Because a state is organized with a legal system, and exists for fair enforcement of laws that people have agreed and pledged to. So, some laws that are out of place with the reality are revised or abrogated. People pay taxes and give salaries to government workers so they can properly fulfill such duties.

A small and strong government

Lecturer: Thanks for your input. In general, the state as a body is perceived as enforcing laws in a neutral manner while keeping itself at a distance from various social forces and interest groups.

In my opinion, one important role of the state is to promote and increase the *public good*. Government is run with taxpayer's money, so it should consider various issues for the public good. For example, medical service, education, energy, water supply, communications, and railway are obviously public goods, as they directly influence people's basic livelihood and pursuit of happiness. So, areas related to these services can best be managed by the state so that individual people may have access to basic services at the least. Starting some time ago, however, there has been a growing voice that calls for *a small and strong government* to reduce the role of the state. In this regard, let me read a piece of writing that I wrote during the presidency of Lee Myung-bak.

Having pushed for reduction of government workforce and privatization of state corporations in the name of a small and efficient government, Lee Myung-bak's government is providing fodder for controversy by pushing for the hardest possible responses to street protests and predicting the operation of a special arrest unit that reminds people of the riot police (called *Baekgoldan*) during the past military dictatorship. The recent steps taken by the Lee Myung-bak government are geared to the single goal of creating *a small and strong government*.

First proposed by former UK prime minister Margaret Thatcher and former US president Ronald Reagan, both notorious advocates of neo-liberalism, *small government* has become the ideal form for all countries that promote neo-liberalism. As South Korea adopted neo-liberalism, its erstwhile governments have equally advocated *a small and strong government*.

The people of South Korea, who have felt dissatisfied with the *state*, are sending inappropriate support (responding to the call for a small and strong government), at the suggestion that they're trying to reduce taxes by creating a smaller and more efficient government and keeping lazy government workers on alert. Then, what is the essence of *small and strong government*?

First of all, what is *small government*?

A small government works to privatize one after another state corporation, those that were previously managed by the government. Education, healthcare, electricity, telecommunications, the railroad, and the water supply are what the Lee Myung-bak government is trying to privatize in the name of *small government*.

Healthcare privatization means providing healthcare as a business opportunity for capital by reducing state healthcare and introducing private healthcare on a large scale. Healthcare for profit. Privatized education is about driving students into no-holds-barred competition for college entrance by giving full autonomy to the college admission process and introducing self-sufficient private high schools, turning the whole education sector into a money game for private educational foundations. Privatizing electricity, telecommunications, the railway, the water supply and so on surrenders those services that were previously provided as public services as business models for capital's pursuit of profit and will end up denying poor people access to such services with exorbitant rate hikes.

Thus, *privatization* is about surrendering the public services of the government to capital as business opportunities.

Small government doesn't stop at privatization. One of their magic spells rests in the words *tax cut*. At first glance, it may look plausible, but that's not the truth. The tax that the Lee Myung-bak government is trying to cut is *total real estate tax*, which people who have accumulated tremendous wealth through real estate speculation simply hate to pay. And the government is going to reduce *income tax* imposed on business people who make a lot of money. Reducing this much tax for rich people, the state is naturally left with smaller tax revenue. Then, the government must reduce its spending, which should lead to a reduction of *welfare benefits* for less wealthy citizens. This is the nature of *tax saving* that the small government trumpets.

The small government which Lee Myung-bak pushes for plans to eliminate the various programs that were introduced for protecting the environment and human rights, all at once, in the name of *deregulation*. Those plans that are being implemented by *the small government* are about surrendering the entire national territory for a money game of capitalists.

Then, what is *the strong government*?

As I said earlier, privatizing through pushing for *a small government*, cutting taxes, and relaxing regulations will inevitably throw the life of the average family and individual, the largest portion of the country's population, into a miserable plight. It ushers in a society where people cannot get the benefits of education, healthcare, electricity, telecommunications, "public transportation", and water — unless they can pay for it, pay whatever price the corporations decide to charge. Welfare programs curtailed in response to tax cuts for rich people will do away with the minimum life support for poor people.

Driven to misery, people will be forced to take to the streets in protest. That's when the strong government is needed. A strong government is mercilessly good at *law enforcement*, wielding clubs and shields against people who have rushed out on the streets out of distresses, while asserting *compliance* and *strict law enforcement*. Otherwise, their rule cannot be maintained. That's why Lee Myung-bak's government wants to bring back *Baekgoldan*.

Small and strong government, a model which is sweeping the world together with neo-liberalism, is in fact a government that couldn't be *smaller* before capital and couldn't be stronger toward workers and grassroots. This is the instruction manual that has been created by the rule of capital, parading as neo-liberalism worldwide.

And it wasn't just Lee Myung-bak. His predecessor, Roh Moo-hyun, was touted as relatively reformist but his government wasn't so different. As a presidential candidate, Roh Moo-hyun pledged that he would help workers. Once he became president, however, he created a law that expanded employment of irregular workers. He even sent troops, joining the US invasion of Iraq, and pushed for the Korea–US FTA. Worse, two farmers were beaten to death by riot police during protest rallies.

All the South Korean governments so far, including Park Geun-hye, have greatly disappointed the Korean people. Most Korean people say, "Politicians are all the same! Rotten!" What on earth is wrong with them?

The State monopolizes violence

Student B: Right, government seems to be stronger toward workers and the grassroots.

Lecturer: Now *strong government* has popped up, let me say one important characteristic of the state. In a class society that is divided into rulers and the ruled, the state is characteristically entitled to an exclusive and lawful use of violence. The military and the police are such organizations affiliated with the state.

There's nobody who thinks that the two world wars were fought in the interests of the workers and grassroots of those countries involved. Countries jockeyed for colonies until they fought each other in the World Wars, when most workers and grassroots bled, conscripted to the military. If people keep firearms in their houses, when the government drives them to wars, those who don't want to shed their blood will take up arms and violently resist the government. Could the rulers accept such a situation? They will never do that.

The state will never share with the ruled its legal and exclusive right to exercise violence for such reasons. Most of the political prisoners that the court locks up are progressives. Conservatives that are nabbed as political prisoners are extremely rare. Defenders of capitalism aren't arrested as political prisoners.

The state that existed before the advent of capitalism still served as a body that realized the interests of the contemporary ruling class. For example, in a slave society, the state guaranteed the right for slave-masters to drive slaves with a law. The leader of the Cuban revolution, Fidel Castro (1926–2016) said in an interview with news media, "Only a super-democratic state such as the Cuban is capable of arming its people." The flip side of this statement is that in a society that is divided between the rulers and the ruled, the government cannot give arms to people. If the capitalist class society allows people to arm themselves, what's going to happen? Wouldn't the society become extremely restless?

Student A: It is very important that the state can lawfully and exclusively use violence. Violence is a powerful means with which the state can impose its will, for it can put into custody people who break the law.

You said, in a slave society, it is legal to keep slaves. In that context, laws in a capitalist society seem to reveal its power structure rather than represent universal truth. But law students tend to regard law as truth that transcends time and history.

Lecturer: Laws can only be products of specific time periods. The capitalist society in which individual persons own land gets a law on land ownership. In a society where land is common property of the whole community, there is no such law to protect individual people's ownership of land.

Rule with legal system and education

Student A: People's view of the state seems to be formed through general education. Schools teach students that the state and the laws are impartial and fair. Come to think of it, it is in fact the state that controls the educational system. We form our perception of the state through education, but the state is in charge of that education.... Don't you smell something fishy here?

Lecturer: That's why the regular curriculum doesn't touch on the content of Marx's critique of political economy. The education system, and the media, focus on a favorable treatment of the capitalist market economy, which is a far cry from what people experience in the real world. The huge gap between rich and poor, irreparable environmental degeneration, exploitation of workers, impoverished farmers...

Schools don't address these serious problems. Junior Achievement (JA Worldwide) and similar organizations offer after-school programs in many communities; they give students practice in creating a company, producing something, marketing it, and selling it. This trains them to think like an entrepreneur. But no one trains them to see how chasing profits leads to cutting corners and taking advantage of others. And while these programs are funded by corporations, foundations and individual donors in the US, in most countries such programs are specifically supported by government.

Student C: In capitalist societies, the government seems to work to strengthen the capitalists' ruling system.

Lecturer: If you see what kind of people make up the Congress, don't you find it natural that the government would be run that way? If the human heart can be won over by money, surely governments can be. Nearly all the members of Congress come from the Establishment or they speak for it. Many of government officials cycle in and out between corporate and government jobs. In capitalist societies, most people are workers, not capitalists; but it isn't easy to find workers or friends of the working class in government. Their legislators don't protect the majority of the population. If half our congressmen were juggling low-paying jobs that offered no benefits, or minimal benefits, don't you think our employee-protection laws would be stronger?

But voters have to change, too. Politicians depend on corporate funding for their campaigns. Ignoring this fact, voters allow candidates to steer election campaigns into debates on superficial issues rather than demanding to know their positions on critical economic and social questions. And they end up voting for people who speak for the capitalists....

While a lot of people envy the welfare available in Northern European countries, they aren't interested in how those countries could have built such societies. In Northern Europe, progressive parties like the Labor Party, the Socialist Party, and the Social Democratic Party came to power and changed the laws and systems.

In the US, the term "Socialism" has been hijacked in order to confuse the matter. Socialism focuses on providing an adequate standard of living for the greatest possible percentage of society, rather than focusing on profit. It aims to provide fairness and equality — that is, equal opportunity. But no one can guarantee equality of outcomes, as we keep hearing about today.

No socio-economic system or government can guarantee that two individuals will do equally well, since cognitive ability and the propensity for hard work cannot be distributed equally; and there's no fairness in penalizing those who do their best in order to reward others who squander their opportunities.

Points to Ponder

- Let's think about the true meaning of a small and strong government.

- Why does the state have a monopoly on violence?
- How do legislators and the education system support adherence to capitalism?

Karl Marx was born in Trier, Germany, on May 5, 1818. He entered the University of Bonn in October 1835. Marx's father wanted his son to study law and become a lawyer like him, but turning a deaf ear on his father's advice, Karl indulged in literature and philosophy. Armed with ardent passions, Karl engaged in fierce debates, never refused a drink, and even wound up participating in a duel. Worried about his son's future, the father transferred Karl to Humboldt University of Berlin, where Karl still remained absorbed in philosophy instead of law. Especially as Humboldt University of Berlin was under the heavy influence of Hegel and his disciples, Karl naturally immersed himself in Hegelian philosophy and actively participated in student activism. (Afterwards, under the influence of Feuerbach, Karl Marx overcame the idealistic character of Hegelian philosophy and established his unique philosophy in dialectic materialism.) After his father passed away on May 10, 1838, Marx applied himself more to the study of philosophy and received a doctoral degree in Philosophy from University of Jena with his dissertation titled "Differenz der demokritischen und epikureischen Naturphilosophie (The Difference between the Democritean and the Epicurean Natural Philosophy)".

Following his graduation, Karl Marx worked as editor of *Rheinische Zeitung*, writing social criticisms as a journalist. When a government clampdown shut down the newspaper, Karl went to France, where he associated with socialists and met his life-time comrade Friedrich Engels (1820–1895). Marx joined Der Bund der Gerechten (League of the Just), a secret society, and when banished by the French government, he moved to Brussels, Belgium.

In 1848, the League of the Just was converting to the Communist League, and in preparing its foundation, Marx wrote the famous *Manifest der Kommunistischen Partei* (*Manifesto of the Communist Party*). In February and March 1848, revolutions broke out in France and Prussia but were soon suppressed. Branded as a dangerous person, Karl Marx exiled himself in London. In England, Marx focused on writing and in 1867, published Volume 1 of *Das Kapital*, a monumental masterpiece in history. However, Marx couldn't complete his *Das Kapital* and died on Mar. 14, 1883. With all due respect to the manuscripts left by Marx, Engels compiled them into Volume 2 and 3 of *Das Kapital*.

*

People living in the 21st-century are thrilled at the sharp analysis of capitalist society that a German thinker encapsulated in words some 150 years ago. It's a real eye-opener.

Recently, in Western society the wealth gap between rich and poor has gaped open wider and wider, while great numbers of people are suffering from the lack of normal jobs, patching together part-time and temp assignments without benefits. In the US, about 50% of the working-age population is considered to be out of the workforce — many because they've given up looking for a job and are no longer qualified to receive unemployment benefits.

Enlightened people alone can break the chains of slaves. If more and more people have their eyes opened, the power of the majority can change the social structure.

Marx left two big philosophical works for humankind. One is *Das Kapital*, which analyzes the capitalist economic system, and the other is his theory on historical materialism, which offers an insight into the law of historical progress from the perspective of dialectical materialism. To get at the essence of the Marxist philosophy, one must fully understand both *Das Kapital* and his thoughts on historical materialism.

In his *Thesen über Feuerbach* (*Theses on Feuerbach*), Marx said, "The philosophers have only interpreted the world in various ways; the point, however, is to change it." True knowledge must lead to action. A society that plunges the majority of its members in despair, sorrow, and distress cannot last.

Hugo Chávez (1954–2013), the late former president of Venezuela, dedicated everything to upholding the cause of '21st-century socialism' against the imperialist United States. He sought to create a society in which not just a few capitalists but the majority of people take the proprietorship. Of course, social progress doesn't realize in a linear fashion. Currently, Venezuela after the death of Chávez and the other countries in the South and Central America are experiencing difficulties as the local Establishment is on its counter-offensive. In the long run, however, human society has clearly made progress through repeated moves forward and backward.

One doesn't have to reap the fruit of the seeds that one sows. Provided that our posterity will reap the fruit, we have sufficient reason to sow seeds today. I write books and give lectures with this conviction. Let me wrap up the book by quoting the well-known line of the former Venezuelan president Hugo Chávez.

"The only way to end poverty is to give power to the poor."

Printed in the United States
By Bookmasters